Hope For

Hurting

Hearts:

A Journey of Healing

Dr. Don Woodard

All Scripture Quotations are from the

Authorized King James Bible

LightKeeper Publications
PO Box 490
Troutville, VA 24175
540-354-8573
csm2va@netzero.net

ISBN-10:1503385817
ISBN-13: 9781503385818

This Book Is Lovingly Dedicated To:

My dear Saviour, Who alone is the true Healer of the brokenhearted;

Faithful caregivers of those who suffer;

*Amber and Rusty—
the Resurrection will be a Reunion!*

Acknowledgements:

A special thank you to Miss Danielle Warden and Mrs. Debbie Black for editing assistance and other valuable input on this project, And my sincere and heartfelt gratitude to the wonderful people of Beacon Baptist Church for giving me the honor of being their pastor.

Cover photograph by:
Megan Weddle
photographybymeganweddle.com

CONTENTS

FOREWORD

Since we first met Dr. Don Woodard about twenty years ago, he has demonstrated a God-given ability to step alongside those who sorrow in order to bring help and comfort. He has been in our church on several occasions, and his compassion was especially comforting after my wife lost her mother due to cancer; I recall the unusual insights he shared with us at that time. Several years later, Dr. Woodard was once again a blessing as he ministered to my family when our 18-year-old son Eric was killed in a car crash. God has given us comforters over the years, and I believe this book is a great resource for all who have suffered a loss and are grieving. As I read the chapters of *Hope for Hurting Hearts*, I saw again in Dr. Woodard's writing a wealth of understanding and direction into that daily comfort afforded to us by the Lord Jesus Christ Himself.

Here is a pastor writing from his heart as well as his life experiences, addressing a need we all will come to eventually: the need for God to lead us through the journey of sorrow. I strongly recommend this practical and doctrinal daily resource, and I will be using it in my ministry in the days ahead.

Dr. Eric M. Tharp, Pastor
Central Valley Baptist Church Manteca, CA

PREFACE

~ A Journal for Your Journey ~

Dear Reader,

The book you now hold in your hands, *Hope for Hurting Hearts: A Journey of Healing,* includes a feature that will enable you to make this volume uniquely and personally yours. After years of ministering to those who are suffering, we have found that a journal can be a valuable tool for working through varied and complex emotions. As we worked on this book, we wanted it to be as helpful to you as possible—whether you are walking through the valley of heartbreak or facing the storm of tribulation; it was with this desire in mind that we included guided journal pages.

Our suggestion to you is that you read one chapter each day, then write down any thoughts you may have regarding the day's reading on the corresponding journal page. After you have completed the initial twenty-one days of reading and journaling, you will find that there are an additional nineteen days of devotional thoughts, along with lines for journal entries. This makes a total of forty days, which I believe is significant: forty is the number of days we find in the Bible for the grieving process, and that number also implies a new beginning. I share this information not as a cold calculation of when your hurting will end, but as a means of encouraging you along this difficult journey.

In order for this book to be of greatest benefit to you, please feel free to highlight thoughts, make notes in the margins, and even re-read any chapters that you feel have especially ministered to your heart.

My prayer is that this book will help you in your journey of healing.

A Servant of the King of Kings,

Dr. Don Woodard

~ Day 1 ~

You Are Not Alone

Have you ever had the dreadful feeling that you were all alone and that no one could relate to what you were experiencing? At some time or another all of us have had those feelings, and when we experience a personal loss or heartache, those feelings of being alone often become part of our grief. I would like to share some truths with you on that very subject and encourage you that "You Are Not Alone"!

I do not know the specifics of the challenges you face, the circumstances of your grief, or the severity of your "storm"; however, I do understand the experience of feeling very much alone and the fear of being abandoned on the sea of life during the darkness of a storm.

Sometimes when we are grieving or dealing with heartbreaking circumstances, we feel as though we are in a small boat in the middle of a vast ocean. It would seem that we are all alone; no one knows where we are, and no one is able to rescue us—to offer us comfort, strength, or security.

We may feel like we are totally out of control, while all around us the storm rages, the thunder rumbles, and the lightning flashes across the blackness of the sky. Our emotions tell us that we are in a place no one else could possibly understand, and we feel hopeless.

My friend you are not alone; there is a similar event as I have just described recorded in the sacred Scriptures. The passage of scripture I'm referring to is Matthew 14:22-34.

> *22) And straightway Jesus constrained his disciples   to get into a ship, and to go before him unto the other side, while he sent the multitudes away.*
> *23) And when he had sent the multitudes away, he went up into a mountain apart to pray: and when the evening was come, he was there alone.*
> *24) But the ship was now in the midst of the sea, tossed with waves: for the wind was contrary.*
> *25) And in the fourth watch of the night Jesus went unto them, walking on the sea.*
> *26) And when the disciples saw him walking on the sea, they were troubled, saying, It is a spirit; an they cried out for fear.*
> *27) But straightway Jesus spake unto them, saying, Be of good cheer; it is I; be not afraid.*

*28) And Peter answered him and said,
Lord, if it be thou, bid me come unto thee
on the water.
29) And he said, Come. And when Peter
was come down out of the ship, he
walked on the water, to go to Jesus.
30) But when he saw the wind
boisterous, he was afraid; and beginning
to sink, he cried, saying, Lord, save me.
31) And immediately Jesus stretched
forth his hand, and caught him, and said
unto him, O thou of little faith, wherefore
didst thou doubt?
32) And when they were come into the
ship, the wind ceased.
33) Then they that were in the ship
came and worshipped him, saying, Of a
truth thou art the Son of God.
34) And when they were gone over, they
came into the   land of Gennesaret.*

There are some powerful principles
underlying this event that can be of great
encouragement to us during the storms of life.
First, notice that the disciples had been
obedient; they were in the ship Jesus Christ
had told them to enter, and they were going to
a place He told them to go. Then suddenly
they found themselves in a storm on the sea!
Often when a storm comes into our lives, we
tend to wonder, "Am I doing what I am

supposed to be doing? Am I in the right place? Am I going in the right direction? Am I in the will of God?" Imagine the disciples questioning themselves in their dangerous situation. Despite the fact that they were in the will of God in every possible way, they were confronted with a terrifying storm!

Friend, if you are facing a storm today, it does not necessarily mean that you are not where you are supposed to be, that you are going in the wrong direction, or that you are out of the will of God. It simply means that **you and I will experience adversity in this life, but we must go on in faith**, trusting the One who sent us on our journey.

Notice also in our Bible passage that the disciples were afraid. Fear is a natural response to many of life's difficulties. The disciples feared the storm, and they feared for their lives. They had no power over the storm, nor could they control their specific circumstances. To make matters worse, they were convinced that no one knew where they were.

Perhaps as you are going through your storm you have those same emotions and concerns. You see lightning flashing across the sky, you hear the thunder, you feel the force of the wind, and you see yourself as that tiny boat on the sea. You are thinking, "No one knows where I am. I'm lost in the emotions of my grief."

Wait a moment; was it true that no one knew where the disciples were? On the contrary—and this is an important truth—Someone *did* know. Jesus Christ knew exactly where the disciples were! No matter how severe your storm is, you are not alone. Our Saviour knows right where you are, both emotionally and in your circumstances.

So far we have seen that the disciples had been obedient when they faced this storm, that they were afraid of a situation that was beyond their control, and that the Lord knew where they were. Now notice something unusual; pay attention to **how** Jesus Christ came to His disciples during this storm. Have you ever wondered why it is recorded in the Bible that our Lord walked on water? I believe this was written not only to affirm once again that Jesus Christ is God and thus He can do what seems impossible to man, but also to remind us that there is no place we can go in life that Christ Himself is unable to go! You may have the feeling that no one can reach you in your storm to comfort and rescue you; on the contrary, my friend, the Lord Jesus Christ can! You are precious to Him, and He is able to do whatever is necessary to help you.

Not only did Jesus know where His disciples were and go to their rescue, but He also stepped into the boat with them. Notice verse thirty-two, *"And when they were come into the ship, the wind ceased."* What a blessing! Our Saviour can find us, wherever we are—no matter how terrible the storm—and He will get in the boat with us! As you go through your storm, you may at times feel alone, but if you look in your boat through the eyes of faith, you will see the Saviour is already there; in His time He will calm your storm.

Think for a moment about the sun. We may not always see it, we may not always feel its warmth, but it is always present. The Lord has promised every believer that He will never leave or forsake us (Hebrews 13:5b). You are not alone. He has reached you in your storm and is already in your boat, along with the power to calm the storm and to reassure your fearful heart.

I want to consider one last truth today; it is found in verse thirty-four, *"And when they were gone over, they came into the land of Gennesaret."* I am so glad God's Word tells us that the disciples survived the storm and arrived at their destination! You will also make it through your storm. You may sustain painful injuries along the way, but God will see you through, and He will bring healing for those hurts. You will arrive at the place God has for you on your journey, because God has a purpose for your life; remember that *the Lord Himself* is traveling with you. It is not possible for you to enter waters where He cannot protect you, and He will never lose you in the storm.

Take heart, my friend; you are not alone on your journey!

Hope for Hurting Hearts Journal

Day 1: You Are Not Alone

Date:_____

Today's Scripture: Psalm 9

"No matter how severe your storm is,
you are not alone. Our Saviour knows
right where you are, both emotionally
and in your circumstances."

From today's reading I learned:_____

_____

_____

_____

_____

_____

On my heart today:_____

_____

_____

_____

~ Day 2 ~

The Next Thing You Do Is Crucial

During this time of difficulty in your life, have you paused to consider how important the very next step you take—or the very next decision you make—could be? From counseling and observing those who have faced great challenges, I cannot emphasize enough that "The Next Thing You Do Is Crucial"!

It is worthwhile in our study to consider the life of Job; here was a man who endured terrible losses and heartache. You are probably familiar with the horrific chain of events that happened to this godly man, so we will just mention them briefly and concentrate instead on Job's responses to what had occurred in his life.

Over one short span of time, four different messengers came to Job with heartbreaking reports. Job had been robbed of all his wealth, he had lost his primary source of income, he had lost most of his servants (employees), and then the unthinkable had happened: his children were all killed when a windstorm caused the house they were gathered in to collapse. To lose a child is devastating, but to lose ten in a single tragedy is more than our minds can comprehend!

In my years of ministry I have met scores of people who have suffered tragedies in their lives, but I have never met anyone who has suffered as

Job did. I have met people who have experienced heartache, but nothing to compare to what Job suffered. Job lost his children, his health, and most of his possessions. As if these circumstances were not distressing enough, his "friends" chose to lecture Job rather than to console him, and even his wife criticized instead of comforting her husband.

You are reading this book because you have found yourself in terrible circumstances, or perhaps you are in a season of grief. You may feel as though you can relate to Job, as you see that his heart was broken over his calamity, just as your heart is broken over your circumstances.

My friend, what you choose to do next is crucial! It will have a lasting impact on your life as you walk through this valley of grief and move on to emotional healing, renewed strength, and for some of you, rebuilding your life. The next thing you do could determine whether you will take the road to victory or the road to defeat; it will lead you to the path of **bettering yourself** or the path of **bitterness**. The next thing you do could determine whether you will travel in the direction of trusting God or that of harboring anger in your heart toward God! Choose victory! Choose bettering yourself! Choose trusting God!

What was Job's reaction? He received the report of his financial losses, and just when he thought things could get no worse, he learned that his precious children were dead. We can learn a great deal from the way Job responded to these reports, as recorded for us in Job 1:20-22:

> *22) Then Job arose, and rent his mantle, and shaved his head, and fell down upon the ground, and worshipped,*
> *21) And said, Naked came I out of my mother's womb, and naked shall I return thither: the LORD gave, and the LORD hath taken away; blessed be the name of the LORD.*
> *22) In all this Job sinned not, nor charged God foolishly.*

Let's take a closer look at what this passage reveals about Job's actions.

1. Job rent his mantle; that is, he tore his garment. In Old Testament days, tearing one's clothing was a symbol of grieving; by doing this, Job was saying that his heart was crushed. The tearing of his garment was an outward expression of his inward sorrow. I cannot begin to imagine the grief Job endured. My friend, it is natural and healthy to grieve; God created us to grieve when we have lost someone dear to us.

2. The Bible tells us that Job also shaved his head, which was a symbol of his humility. In Job's day and throughout the Old Testament period it was common to shave the heads of

slaves in order to remind them of their proper place; they were to be in submission to the authority of their masters in every aspect of their lives. Job was expressing that he had no pride or glory in and of himself. He was demonstrating his total submission to his God, even though he did not understand what the Lord was allowing to happen in his life. Job was expressing his humility before God, as well as his recognition that he was God's servant.

3. Then Job <u>fell to the ground and worshipped.</u> He said, *"Blessed be the name of the LORD."* That word "blessed" means "sanctified" or "set apart"; it can also have other meanings, such as "lovely" or "happy"—that which brings joy. Job had the right heart attitude toward God and his circumstances. His attitude was that although he had suffered this terrible heartbreak, the name of God should be revered because His name is "set apart" from all others! Job was also acknowledging that, despite his pain, the name of the Lord was still lovely to him! Job worshipped the Lord and surrendered his heart to Him. He knew that somehow, at some time, he would again experience joy if he kept His focus on the Lord.

My friend, when Job received the reports of his great loss, he could have shaken his fist toward Heaven and cursed God. He could have gone into a rage of anger, and he could have allowed his heart to become bitter. Instead, Job chose to have faith in God throughout his turmoil, because he recognized that how he responded to his circumstances was of great importance.

Perhaps you have received some terrible report, and you are in the valley of decision. I implore you to think carefully before you take action, because the next thing you do is crucial! The way you respond in word or deed will have repercussions. What will you do next? I would like to offer a few suggestions for your consideration.

➤ Assess your circumstances.
What has taken place? What decisions need your attention? What options are available to you, and what resources for counsel do you have, such as your pastor, your church family, or reliable friends? By "reliable," I am referring to someone whom you trust implicitly. It should be someone who believes the Bible, who prays for you and has your best interest at heart. Such individuals as these I have mentioned can help you develop a plan of action for the future.

➤ Make no "big" decisions immediately.
Over the years we have seen people confronted with grief who have quit their

jobs, sold their homes, or left a church because they were hurting and were not thinking clearly. Those decisions were emotional ones and in most instances brought eventual regret. Unless it is something that actually **requires** an immediate decision, give yourself time to heal, to pray, and to think.

➤ Trust God with your grief.
Grieving is natural, healthy, and necessary, but we must not abandon our faith in God; trust Him in this time of grief. Your walk with God is vital—take time to speak with Him in prayer and to listen as He speaks to you through His Word. For most of us, dark days may not be the best time to tackle a prophetic Old Testament book or to start a complex Bible study; sometimes the most soothing thing we can do for our souls is to "live" in the book of Psalms for awhile, and to allow the Holy Spirit to do a work in our hearts. Keep trusting God!

➤ Worship the Lord.
Surrender yourself and your situation to the Lord. Things may look grim right now, but the name of Jesus Christ is still blessed; He is worthy of our worship and praise, even when we are going through a valley. His

name is still lovely, and He alone can restore our joy!

 Determine in your heart not to become bitter.
Allow the Lord to make you *better* through and in spite of your circumstances.

 Stay close to people who will be supportive.
Avoid people who will discourage you or possibly criticize you. Not everyone who knows you will understand what you are going through, and many of your closest friends will mean well but may make inappropriate comments, or possibly even say hurtful things. They do not do this intentionally; they simply do not know how to respond to you or to your circumstances, so they say what they think is helpful, but often it is not. It will be best for you to stay close to people who will encourage you: people who will build you up rather than tear you down. You will need to have people around you who will help you in the healing process.

My friend, whatever your circumstances are, "The Next Thing You Do Is Crucial"!

Seek counsel, give yourself time before making important decisions, keep walking with God, and spend time with people who will truly help you.

God bless you on your journey, and remember: *"blessed be the name of the LORD"*!

Hope for Hurting Hearts Journal

Day 2: The Next Thing You Do Is Crucial

Date:_____

Today's Scripture: Psalm 42

"My friend, what you choose to do next
is crucial! It will have a lasting impact
on your life as you walk through this
valley of grief and move on to emotional
healing, renewed strength, and for some
of you, rebuilding your life."

From today's reading I learned:_____

_____

_____

_____

_____

_____

On my heart today:_____

_____

~ Day 3 ~

There Is Hope

It is vital that you grasp this! No matter what your heartbreak or circumstances are, "There Is Hope," and that hope is available to you! In the beginning of Jesus Christ's earthly ministry, He went to the synagogue and stood among the congregation to read from the book of Isaiah. We find this recorded in Luke 4:18 and 19; Jesus said,

> 18) *The Spirit of the Lord is upon me, because he hath anointed me to preach the gospel to the poor; he hath sent me to heal the brokenhearted, to preach deliverance to the captives, and recovering of sight to the blind, to set at liberty them that are bruised,*
> 19) *To preach the acceptable year of the Lord.*

This passage offers comfort and encouragement to those who are hurting. Notice the phrase at the end of verse eighteen: *"them that are bruised"*. The word *"bruised"* means something has been crushed, hurt, or broken. These words accurately describe our emotional state when we are carrying a heavy burden that seems to be crushing us. The verse also contains

the phrase *"to set at liberty"*; this means that
there is hope of being set free!

Perhaps your heart is crushed, hurting, and
broken. You may feel that you will never be free
from the burdens that trouble you, but the Lord,
in His time, will set you free from those burdens.

You may say, "Yes, He will one day set me free
from my burdens, but what about my broken
heart? It seems that I will have this hurt forever."
Notice the verse again. Jesus also said, *"He,*
[referring to God the Father] *hath sent me to heal
the broken hearted"*. My friend, there is hope and
healing for your life: Jesus Christ is the Mender
and Healer of the brokenhearted. He understands
your circumstances and the emotions you are
experiencing right now. In His time He will heal
your broken heart, if you will allow Him to do so.
Consider this comparison:

If you or I have a broken arm, we should get
prompt medical attention. The doctor, possibly a
bone specialist, would take certain steps in
treating the injury.

> ➤ He would x-ray the arm to find the exact
> location of the break. Let me reassure you
> that Jesus Christ has already done that!
> He knows the exact "place" where your
> heart is broken—that is, He knows what
> has occurred in your life, and He
> understands your pain. He is a
> "Specialist" in all that concerns your life.

- The doctor would then set your broken arm so it would mend properly. The Saviour wants do all that is necessary to ensure that your heart will mend. He will use various "treatments," such as the sweet counsel of caring friends, and even the gradual passing of time under His watchful eye, to bring about your healing.

- The doctor may also have some medications for you to take, to help you with the healing process. The Saviour has some prescriptions for you as well. The Word of God can ease the pain and help with the healing process, much like a soothing balm. Meditating on specific portions of Scripture and talking with the Lord in prayer are all necessary "medicines" as we work through our difficulties and emotional hurts.

- Lastly, the doctor would no doubt ask that you rest your arm, and not overexert it while it is healing. During your heart's healing process you may need to rest your emotions, your spirit, and your mind. In this part of your healing journey, it is wise to avoid unnecessary situations that could be emotionally draining.

Now, if you really had broken your arm, you would sincerely want and need a doctor to help you; you would listen carefully to what he had to say, and you would follow his advice. Certainly when you and I have a broken heart, we should heed the advice of the Great Physician! Remember what the Lord read there in the temple? He said that God the Father had sent Him to *"heal the broken hearted...to set at liberty them that are bruised."*

There is hope! Regardless of what you are facing, there is hope! Our Lord, our Great Physician, can help you; He loves you and desires to give you healing in your spirit. There may be a "scar" once the healing is complete, but just like a physical scar, the pain will gradually come to an end. As you walk with the Lord each day, He will help you to regain your strength so that you can once again live a victorious Christian life!

There is hope because there is a Healer of the brokenhearted, and His name is Jesus Christ! Trust Him with your broken heart, and follow the prescriptions found in His Word. Meditate on His promises! As you spend time talking to the Lord in prayer, ask for His healing, strength, and guidance. There is healing for your hurts because Jesus Christ is the Healer of the brokenhearted.

God bless you on your journey!

HOPE

HOPE is a word that lightens a load;
HOPE shines a light down a dark road.
HOPE is a word that brings a smile;
HOPE makes life more worthwhile.
HOPE is a word that spreads some cheer
HOPE knows that Jesus is near.
HOPE is a word that someone may need;
HOPE can help to plant a seed.
HOPE is a word that has great power;
HOPE comes through in the darkest hour.
HOPE is a word that never ends;
HOPE is always our dearest friend.
HOPE is a word Jesus knows best;
HOPE kept my Saviour through His test.
HOPE is a word that conquers my fear;
HOPE lives on because Jesus is near.
HOPE is a word that never grows old;
HOPE is far dearer than gold.
HOPE is a word so precious to me;
HOPE is all I expected it to be.

~Rebecca Warden

Hope for Hurting Hearts Journal

Day 3: There Is Hope

Date:_____

Today's Scripture: Psalm 16

"My friend, there is hope and healing for
your life: Jesus Christ is the Mender
and Healer of the broken- hearted."

*From today's reading I learned:*_____

_____

_____

_____

_____

_____

*On my heart today:*_____

_____

_____

_____

~ Day 4 ~

The Juniper Tree

There are times that you and I read something in Scripture and we may question why it is there. Such is the case in I Kings chapter nineteen, where we find the prophet Elijah sitting under a lowly juniper tree. Have you ever wondered, why a juniper?

Elijah had just experienced a supernatural victory on Mt. Carmel and had witnessed a sweeping national revival as Israel turned away from Baal and back to Jehovah. Certainly Elijah should have been on "shouting ground"!

Instead, Elijah is running for his life. Queen Jezebel, angered over the events of Mt. Carmel, had sent word to Elijah that she would have him killed in twenty-four hours. Victory turned to despair! The prophet was so depressed and distraught that he asked God to let him die. He wandered, no doubt aimlessly, and arrived in the wilderness, where he sat under a juniper tree.

The wilderness part of Elijah's circumstances is important, for we know that the word "wilderness" in Scripture is usually applied to the desert regions. In addition, "wilderness" can have the meaning of a state of disorder and confusion. I believe that both uses of the word apply to this passage.

Elijah had no definite course of action. He did not seem to know which way to go. Because of his lack of direction, Elijah wandered into the wilderness; his state of mind was no doubt one of confusion, and his life seemed to be in total disorder. We read in I Kings 19:3-4,

> 3) *And when he saw that, he arose, and went for his life, and came to Beersheba, which belongeth to Judah, and left his servant there.*
> 4) *But he himself went a day's journey into the wilderness, and came and sat down under a juniper tree: and he requested for himself that he might die; and said, It is enough; now, O LORD, take away my life; for I am not better than my fathers.*

What about that juniper tree? The juniper that we read of here is not like the varieties of juniper we find in much of the Midwest and eastern United States. Junipers here, given enough rainfall, can grow to be a towering tree. However, in the Middle East, the juniper is found in desert areas; with limited water available, the "tree" is more of a wiry shrub, looking peculiarly like an inverted broom, which resulted in the name "juniper," which literally means "broom." Now that may seem of little consequence as we deal with Elijah's hopeless situation, but think about this for a moment. What would be more hopeless than using a broom to sweep the sand away if you lived in the desert? God's Word is rich with so many comparisons! For Elijah, life itself seemed hopeless, and death was all he could hope for; it would be better, he thought, to die at the hand of His God rather than the wicked Jezebel. Finding a solution to his problem seemed impossible!

Notice also that this worthless little shrub was virtually all he had for shade or hope of sustenance. Elijah could not very easily rest under the shade of an olive tree or a sycamore since he had wandered into the barrenness of a desert area. The prophet could not even dig up part of the juniper root and eat it, because juniper roots are poisonous! We can almost hear the sighing of the man of God as he grieves over his sad and hopeless plight.

The juniper tree is a vivid picture of the place you and I can wander to during a time of grief or sorrow. It is a place where we feel all is hopeless, and life seems futile. If we dare linger in that dangerous place, we may be tempted to "partake" of the juniper, and as a result we will become poisoned within; that poison will eventually spill over, adversely affecting our perspective, our plans, and the people who are dearest to us.

As Elijah rested in the shade of the juniper, he saw himself as having no value for himself or anyone else; it was this, I believe, rather than just fear, that caused him to despair of life itself.

Fortunately for Elijah, in the midst of his turmoil and wrong thinking, he did something that was very right: he cried out to God for help! In his discouragement he cried out and told God of his bleak and impossible circumstances. Elijah's prayer reveals the state of his mind and heart: *"O, LORD, take away my life; for I am not better than my fathers"* (I Kings 19:4b).

Elijah was in a bad situation. However, even though he apparently did not see any value in Himself, God did. Notice the next few verses:

5) *And as he lay and slept under a juniper tree, behold, then an angel touched him, and said unto him, Arise and eat.*
6) *And he looked, and, behold, there was a cake baken on the coals, and a cruse of water at his head. And he did eat and drink, and laid him down again.*
7) *And the angel of the LORD came again the second time, and touched him, and said, Arise and eat; because the journey is too great for thee.*
8) *And he arose, and did eat and drink, and went in the strength of that meat forty days and forty nights unto Horeb the mount of God.*

Because of the value God saw in His servant, He saw that Elijah's most urgent physical needs were met; first we see that Elijah drifted off to sleep for some much-needed physical rest. Then the Lord provided sustenance for him; Elijah was awakened by the Angel of the Lord and given cakes to eat and water to drink. After taking of this refreshment Elijah lay down again for further rest. In verse seven we see the Angel of the Lord touch Elijah and tell him to eat again, *"because the journey is too great for thee."*

Notice with me some important principles in this passage—principles that will encourage you!

> ➤ God saw value in Elijah even though Elijah did not see value in himself. My friend, God sees value in you, no matter what your circumstances are. When we are in a place of sorrow, God still sees our potential, because He placed it within us!

> ➤ Notice that God sent the heavenly messenger to minister to Elijah. I personally believe *"the Angel of the LORD"* was Jesus Christ prior to Bethlehem. The Angel represents another world, the spiritual realm. This world of ours has its tribulations, but in Heaven all is well! Sometimes we need the communication of the heavenly, so we can deal with the disorder, heartaches, and troubles of this world.

- God will minister to your emotional and spiritual needs when you call out to Him.

- God may send you a "heavenly messenger". By that I mean God will send people to encourage your heart. Be sure to drink of the emotional and spiritual refreshment they offer you.

- The journey is difficult. *"...Arise and eat; because the journey is too great for thee."* The journey you are on is a challenging one; you may be in the wilderness now, but you do not have to stay there! After Elijah had some rest and nourishment, he left the juniper tree and continued on to the mount of the Lord. You can also move on in your journey from the juniper tree to hope, peace, and renewed strength on the mount of the Lord.

Journey to Recovery

- The Angel of the Lord touched Elijah, and straightway Elijah received the physical, emotional, and spiritual strength he needed to continue on in his journey.

Are you sitting under the juniper tree today, my friend? God still has a purpose for your life, and you are of great value to Him! He wants to bring you out of the wilderness, away from the juniper tree, and onto the mountain where you can hear the whisper of His voice.

May I make a suggestion to you today? <u>Tell God where it hurts</u>. Call out to Him if you are discouraged, and let Him minister to you. Avoid taking on any projects today. Put everything you can aside and spend time in prayer. Spend time in the Word of God and allow the Lord to work in your heart; let Him give you the strength you need to go on. Ask the Lord to give you a heavenly messenger to encourage you, if that is what He knows is needed. Possibly He has already placed someone in your life that you know you can confide in; contact that person if you feel led to do so, and let him be a blessing to you. That is what brothers and sisters in Christ are for!

May God bless you in this part of your journey; take time to rest in Him along the way!

Hope for Hurting Hearts Journal

Day 4: The Juniper Tree

Date:_____

Today's Scripture: Psalm 139

"God still has a purpose for your life,
and you are of great value to Him! He
wants to bring you out of the
wilderness, away from the juniper tree,
and onto the mountain where you can
hear the whisper of His voice."

*From today's reading I learned:*_____

_____

_____

_____

_____

_____

*On my heart today:*_____

_____

~ Day 5 ~

Be Strong

There is a harsh reality in life: sometimes circumstances demand that we muster inner strength, even when we are uncertain of how to begin and we feel that we do not possess the ability to "Be Strong"! There are times that people whom we love and respect—people we have depended on—either disappoint us or are called home to Heaven, and we wonder how we can ever have sufficient strength to go on with our lives.

Such was the case with Joshua, who suddenly found himself thrust into a position that demanded great strength of character and endurance. Moses, Joshua's leader and mentor, had died. God chose Joshua to take Moses' place and lead the nation of Israel into Canaan, the promised-land. I cannot fully grasp the emotions and the stress Joshua was experiencing as the person he had followed, the one upon whom he leaned for emotional strength, encouragement, and spiritual guidance, was now gone. Those responsibilities that had belonged to Moses were now placed upon Joshua's shoulders.

Turning back was not an option, for behind him was the wilderness in which the nation of Israel had wandered for forty years. The path before him led across the Jordan River, which at that time of year was overflowing its banks; yet somehow Joshua had to confront this seemingly impossible obstacle. He had to go forward to reach their desired destination. We find Joshua and his dilemma recorded in Scripture in Joshua 1:1-9.

1) *Now after the death of Moses the servant of the LORD it came to pass, that the LORD spake unto Joshua the son of Nun, Moses' minister, saying,*
2) *Moses my servant is dead; now therefore arise, go over this Jordan, thou, and all this people, unto the land which I do give to them, even to the children of Israel.*
3) *Every place that the sole of your foot shall tread upon,   that have I given unto you, as I said unto Moses.*
4) *From the wilderness and this Lebanon even unto the great river, the river Euphrates, all the land of the Hittites, and unto the great sea toward the going down of the sun, shall be your coast.*
5) *There shall not any man be able to stand before thee all the days of thy life: as I was with Moses, so I will be with thee: I will not fail thee, nor forsake thee.*
6) *Be strong and of a good courage: for unto this people shalt thou divide for an inheritance the land, which I sware unto their fathers to give them.*

7) *Only be thou strong and very courageous, that thou mayest observe to do according to all the law, which Moses my servant commanded thee: turn not from it to the right hand or to the left, that thou mayest prosper whithersoever thou goest.*
8) *This book of the law shall not depart out of thy mouth; but thou shalt meditate therein day and night, that thou mayest observe to do according to all that is written therein: for then thou shalt make thy way prosperous, and then thou shalt have good success.*
9) *Have not I commanded thee? Be strong and of a good courage; be not afraid, neither be thou dismayed: for the LORD thy God is with thee whithersoever thou goest.*

What an encouraging passage of Scripture! Notice that before God told Joshua to "be strong" in verse six, He made three promises in verses three through five.

> ➤ God promised to give Joshua and the children of Israel all the land they walked upon. The Lord described to Joshua what the major boundaries of this vast area would be.

➤ He promised that no man could successfully stand in opposition to Joshua as long as he lived.

➤ Finally, He promised Joshua, *"As I was with Moses, so I will be with thee, I will not fail thee, not forsake thee."*

In verses six and seven, then again in verse nine, God tells Joshua to *"be strong."* Years ago I was studying this passage of Scripture and wondered why God would make a point of saying this three times. It certainly was not because God's words could not be trusted! I have come to the conclusion it must have been because Joshua needed that reassurance; he had to believe in his own heart that, as a servant of God, he could be strong! Notice that in each of the three instances God said, "Be strong"; in our English language, we would say that God spoke in imperative sentences, expressing a serious command as he sought to instill confidence in His new leader. He was challenging and encouraging him to be strong in his own spirit—in his resolve to do what was needed.

God desires you and me to "be strong" as well. I do not know the specifics or the severity of your circumstances, but my guess is like Joshua you have people who are depending on you. Although you may have suffered a loss or other disappointment, going backward is not an option.

You must go forward, no matter how daunting a task that may seem to you.

If you will take a look around you, you will see people who need you; you will soon realize you need them as well. If you look before you, you will see a Jordan to cross and a Canaan of your own to conquer. Our God still says, *"I will not fail thee, nor forsake thee."*
Believe that this promise of God is for you today, just as it was for Joshua many years ago.

There is one more thing God told Joshua to do, and I want to encourage you with this final thought from Joshua 1:2: *"now therefore arise, go over this Jordan...unto the land which I give to them...."* Arise, my friend! Confront your circumstances! *"Be strong and of a good courage"*! Know that God is with you; He will not leave you or forsake you!

Have faith, my friend! God will give you strength for your journey!

Hope for Hurting Hearts Journal

Day 5: Be Strong

Date:_____

Today's Scripture: Psalm 18

"Although you may have suffered a loss
or other disappointment, going
backward is not an option. You must go
forward, no matter how daunting a task
that may seem to you."

From today's reading I learned:_____

_____

_____

_____

_____

_____

On my heart today:_____

_____

_____

~ Day 6 ~

The Place Of Healing

Beginning in the days of our childhood, we collect memories of special places. Some of these we fondly recall because of an exciting event that took place, while others represent times of victory.

In my years of ministry and counseling people I have noticed that, in stark contrast to those "special places" we remember, location is of little or no consequence as it relates to trouble and broken hearts. Illness, loss of a loved one, feelings of emptiness or being powerless can occur anywhere.

There is one place that *is* of great significance, however, particularly at such low times in our lives: it is the place of healing. It is where you and I must go in order to be spiritually and emotionally refreshed and renewed. Where is this "place"? Of course, I speak symbolically, yet this place is nevertheless very real. By way of illustration, let us look at a passage of Scripture, John 5:1-14, where we read of "a certain man" who had a serious, debilitating infirmity.

> 1) *After this there was a feast of the Jews; and Jesus went up to Jerusalem.*

2) *Now there is at Jerusalem by the sheep market a pool, which is called in the Hebrew tongue Bethesda, having five porches.*

3) *In these lay a great multitude of impotent folk, of blind, halt, withered, waiting for the moving of the water.*

4) *For an angel went down at a certain season into the pool, and troubled the water: whosoever then first after the troubling of the water stepped in was made whole of whatsoever disease he had.*

5) *And a certain man was there, which had an infirmity thirty and eight years.*

6) *When Jesus saw him lie, and knew that he had been now a long time in that case, he saith unto him, Wilt thou be made whole?*

7) *The impotent man answered him, Sir, I have no man, when the water is troubled, to put me into the pool: but while I am coming, another steppeth down before me.*

8) *Jesus saith unto him, Rise, take up thy bed, and walk.*

9) *And immediately the man was made whole, and took up his bed, and walked: and on the same day was the Sabbath.*

10) *The Jews therefore said unto him that was cured, It is the Sabbath day: it is not lawful for thee to carry thy bed.*
11) *He answered them, He that made me whole, the same said unto me, Take up thy bed, and walk.*
12) *Then asked they him, What man is that which said unto thee, Take up thy bed, and walk?*
13) *And he that was healed wist not who it was: for Jesus had conveyed himself away, a multitude being in that place.*
14) *Afterward Jesus findeth him in the temple, and said unto him, Behold, thou art made whole: sin no more, lest a worse thing come unto thee.*

I realize this passage is dealing with a physical infirmity, while we are speaking about infirmities of the heart, but the principles in this passage are both helpful and healing in matters of the heart as well. Clearly, man was created as a spiritual, emotional, and physical being—and these are closely intertwined.

When referring to a "place" of healing, we are not speaking of a mere physical place, but an emotional and spiritual place. The man in the previous passage was at a physical place called the Pool of Bethesda, which means "house of mercy." This was a physical place that certainly had a spiritual significance!

The waters of Bethesda were known to have mysterious healing properties; even those who were seriously ill could be made well by getting into the water—if a certain condition was met. Scripture tells us that *"an angel went down at a certain season into the pool, and troubled the water."* Whoever entered the pool immediately after the angel stirred the water was healed of his or her infirmity. So we find this man at the right place: the place of healing!

[handwritten margin note: Troubled Waters is Healing]

As I have counseled people over the years, many have told me they wanted help, or we could say "spiritual healing." I would prayerfully do my best to give them guidance from the Bible, only to discover that some of these hurting people would not leave the emotional "place" where they were struggling to journey to a place of healing! In other words, as this relates to our Scripture passage, they were unwilling for me to lead them to the Pool of Bethesda.

My desire, and truly the purpose of this book, is to help you journey to the Pool of Bethesda. I want to help you reach the place of spiritual and emotional healing.

As we look further at these verses, we learn that this man had suffered with his infirmity thirty-eight years; that is a long time to carry a burden! He told the Lord, *"I have no man when the water is troubled to put me in the pool"*; we can conclude from his statement that this man had severe physical limitations. He undoubtedly had to have someone carry him to Bethesda, or perhaps he had some-how dragged himself there.

I have traveled to the country of Haiti several times; it is a very poor country, and the average physically challenged person does not own or even have access to a wheelchair. I have seen adults and children who were unable to walk literally drag themselves along the ground. It is a heartbreaking sight! I can imagine the man in John chapter five dragging himself with determination to the Pool of Bethesda, hoping to be healed.

It is the same for us with our emotional infirmities. We must be determined in our hearts to get to the place of healing. The journey will not be an easy one; however, no matter how severe our infirmity might be, there is a spiritual place where the water is stirred by the presence of God, and healing is available! The man in our passage of Scripture had faith in the Pool of Bethesda—in the healing power of the stirred water. He believed healing was possible and no doubt had witnessed the healing of others.

My friend, healing for the wounds of your heart is possible. Many other people down through time have suffered infirmities of the heart and have made their way to the Lord, the ultimate "Place" of healing! You see, as beautiful as the

Pool of Bethesda may have been, it possessed no healing power of its own. It was not until the angel came—God's messenger—that hope and help were possible. This messenger of hope represented God's presence, and it was God Who gave the water this power to heal. Have faith that the Lord is present in the midst of your suffering! You must not quit! You must not lose hope!

You and I can read books, strive to think positively, or try any number of things in hopes of receiving emotional strength, but unless we open our hearts in faith to God's presence through His love, His grace, and the healing power of His Word, we will not realize the full potential of what He can do in our lives.

This truth about the presence of God and His healing ability is unmistakably demonstrated by this fact: once the Lord Jesus Christ was present, the Pool of Bethesda was no longer needed! The Lord did not help the man get into the water; He simply spoke these words: *"Rise, take up thy bed, and walk."* At the **Word** of Jesus Christ the man was made whole. There was no longer a need for the angel to trouble the water, because the One Who was sent to heal the brokenhearted had spoken, and the man with the infirmity heard and obeyed the Word of God! Because he had faith in what the Lord had said, he found the healing he had so desperately needed.

No matter what your infirmity, heartache, trial, or challenge may be, placing your faith in the Bible is essential to your healing.

My friend, the place of healing is a spiritual place. It is being in the place of trusting God and of trusting His Word; it is the place of prayer and worship, and of surrendering our burdens into His care. It is the place where the waters of your soul are not troubled, but calmed. It is the place where you know Christ is present in your soul and that His words bring comfort, strength, healing and peace to your heart.

God bless you on your journey! Let me encourage you to walk in God's Word today.

Hope for Hurting Hearts Journal

Day 6: The Place of Healing

Date:_____

Today's Scripture: Psalm 61

"The journey will not be an easy one;
however, no matter how severe our
infirmity might be, there is a spiritual
place where the water is stirred by the
presence of God, and healing is
available!"

*From today's reading I learned:*_____

_____

_____

_____

_____

_____

*On my heart today:*_____

_____

~ Day 7 ~

The Seasons Change

For years now I have particularly enjoyed watching the changing seasons. Spring, summer, autumn, winter—each season gradually flows into the next, sharing with us its unique characteristics and beauty, as well as telling us of a wise Creator.

By God's design, summer does not abruptly end and usher in autumn. Here where we live in southwestern Virginia, we begin to notice little "signals" such as gradually cooler temperatures and less daylight hours. Soon subtle tints of color appear and begin to spread across the trees along the Blue Ridge Mountains. Autumn has arrived, but change is still coming. Before long there is more of a sharpness in the wind as the temperatures become cooler still; the leaves lose all their color, and we are greeted with feathery frost on our windowpanes as well as snow covering the ground. Winter is here, and we begin to look forward with anticipation to the coming of spring again. This cycle we know as the changing of the seasons repeats itself every year.

This brings us to a very precious portion of Scripture found in Ecclesiastes chapter three. Occasionally I am asked to read this passage at funerals and in some circumstances I have chosen it as my text for a memorial service. I encourage you to read through this passage carefully, taking in every word.

> 1) *To everything there is a season, and a time to every purpose under the heaven:*
> 2) *A time to be born, and a time to die; a time to plant, and a time to pluck up that which is planted;*
> 3) *A time to kill, and a time to heal; a time to break down, and a time to build up;*
> 4) *A time to weep, and a time to laugh; a time to mourn, and a time to dance....*

Verse one tells us, *"To everything there is a season, and a time to every purpose under the heaven."* Just as there are seasons in nature by God's design, so you and I will experience different seasons in our lives.

No matter what circumstances you are facing, whether it is grieving the loss of a loved one or your heart has been broken by other events that have taken place in your life, there is a season for you to walk through. Perhaps we would say it is a time of winter, since in most places wintertime is a cold and dark season. There is a season for the grieving process—a time of healing and renewing our emotional and spiritual strength. I like to refer to this time as the "returning to life process."

In this passage in Ecclesiastes the word "season" means a fitting time, an appointed or appropriate time. When you or I have experienced any kind of devastating situation, it is important that we have a season of grieving—of allowing our emotions to take their course. As the passage in Ecclesiastes tells us clearly, *"To everything there is a season, and a time to every purpose under the heaven, ...A time to weep...(and) a time to mourn...."*

God created us with tears and emotions. He knew we would need to express our emotions, even those of sadness; and as we discussed earlier, He sent Jesus Christ to heal our broken hearts.

Just as it takes time for the body to heal from an illness, so it also takes time for our emotions to heal from sorrow and grief. It requires a season: a period of time for our emotions to be healed and our strength to be renewed.

We discussed earlier that as one season gradually ends, another is beginning. Our season of sorrow is not forever! It will fade into the season of healing. Our season of planting must turn to a season of harvesting; our breaking down must turn to a season of building up. Our season of weeping must turn to a season of laughter, and our season of mourning must turn to a season of rejoicing.

Earth does not remain in one constant season. If it did—let us say that it was always summer—it actually would be unhealthy for all of us; without the dormant period of winter, much of our vegetation, as well as many of our animals, probably would not survive. Many of the germs that cause illness would not be deterred by severe cold, and there would be more sickness.

Similarly, for you to remain in the season of grief is unhealthy for your body, soul and spirit. You must do all that the season you are in calls for; if you are in the season of grief, or the season of sorrow, do all that is necessary and biblical for the renewing of your strength and for the mending of your emotions. You need this time, as mentioned earlier; you need to let your emotions take their course. God created us to do so!

However, it is also important to keep in mind something that most of us do during the seasons of nature: we always plan for the next season. It is interesting that during the winter season we often talk about the flower gardens we will plant in the spring.

Springtime comes and we begin planning our summer activities, vacations, reunions and special projects. By late summer we are talking about how we look forward to the changing of the colors of the leaves and the projects we can do when autumn comes and the weather is cooler. Even when we are enjoying the season we are in, we are usually looking forward to the next season.

As you go through your current season, whether it is a season of grieving, sorrow, healing, or mending of a broken heart, whatever your season might be, look forward! Begin planning what you will do on the other side of this season. If this is a cold and dark season for you, plan something for the emotional season of spring; gradually let go of the season in which you find yourself, and begin walking into the season of spring! There are flower gardens to plant; there are people to whom you can be a blessing. There is rejoicing and there is laughter ahead in the season of spring. There will be warmth, springtime rain, and rainbows to enjoy. The leaves will begin to take their places in the trees, and the pleasant aroma of spring will encourage your heart.

My friend, do not prolong your season of sorrow; let the precious Saviour lead you, little by little, into the season of laughter and rejoicing. Begin now to plan for the good seasons ahead.

God bless you; look forward on your journey!

Hope for Hurting Hearts Journal

Day 7: The Seasons Change

Date:_____

Today's Scripture: Psalm 136

"Our season of weeping must turn to
our season of laughter, and our season
of mourning must turn to a season of
rejoicing."

*From today's reading I learned:*_____

_____

_____

_____

_____

_____

*On my heart today:*_____

_____

_____

_____

~ Day 8 ~

Look For The Beauty

Have you ever been admiring something beautiful such as a painting, some lovely glassware, or perhaps a rare antique when you suddenly noticed a flaw? If we are not careful, we can become so distracted and disturbed by the flaw that we allow it to spoil our enjoyment of the object altogether.

That is true in our lives as well; when we are going through times of sorrow, challenging situations, or disappointments, we can allow them to taint our perspective. The result is something very dangerous, and that is bitterness! We must guard against this stealthy intruder, because it can grow into something deadly. We can become bitter toward God, toward the people around us, and even toward life in general!

Someone wisely said, "Bitterness is the only chemical that destroys its own container." That statement is very true. Over the years I have met so many people who have allowed circumstances to turn their hearts bitter and cold; in reality, their bitterness has done far more damage than the difficult situation they endured!

Whatever you may be confronted with at this time in your life, it is extremely important that you guard against this formidable enemy that can destroy your life. Instead, I want to challenge and encourage you to "Look for the Beauty"!

The Apostle Paul was a man that had plenty of reasons to harbor bitterness in his heart; as Paul wrote his part of our Bible under the inspiration of the Holy Spirit, he penned these words of encouragement and warning in the book of Hebrews: *"Looking unto Jesus the author and finisher of our faith; who for the joy that was set before him endured the cross, despising the shame, and is set down at the right hand of the throne of God"* (Hebrews 12:2).

"Looking unto Jesus"—what wonderful advice for the Christian! Next we will examine a nearby passage in verses 11-15:

> 11) *Now no chastening for the present seemeth to be joyous, but grievous: nevertheless afterward it yieldeth the peaceable fruit of righteousness unto them which are exercised thereby.*
> 12) *Wherefore lift up the hands which hang down, and the feeble knees;*
> 13) *And make straight paths for your feet, lest that which is lame be turned out of the way; but let it rather be healed.*
> 14) *Follow peace with all men, and holiness, without which no man shall see the Lord:*
> 15) *Looking diligently lest any man fail of the grace of God; lest any root of*

*bitterness springing up trouble you, and
thereby many be defiled....*

Once again notice in verse two that Paul
admonishes us with the words *"Looking unto
Jesus"*. I believe in verse fifteen when he writes
"Looking diligently" he is referring back to that
statement, *"Looking unto Jesus"!* It is a reminder
to us that when hardships come in any form we
must look, not casually, but *diligently*, unto the
Lord Jesus Christ, because He is the source of
our faith, as well as our salvation, from beginning
to end! Knowing that we can look to Christ
Himself through the eyes of faith offers us hope,
courage, and confidence! *"Being confident of this
very thing, that he which hath begun a good work
in you will perform it until the day of Jesus Christ"*
(Philippians 1:6).

Look again at verse fifteen of our passage.
Paul says, *"Looking diligently, lest any man fail of
the grace of God."* The phrase *"fail of the grace of
God"* should rivet our attention. Here the Lord is
reminding us that He is our source of grace, and
we know that His grace is limitless! However, if we
do not keep our eyes on the Lord, we will not be
thinking of having access to His grace! Think of it
this way. If I receive a check from someone, that
little piece of paper may represent a great deal of
money. If I carelessly leave the check at home in a
desk drawer, I could possibly even forget about it
altogether. Although that money is mine, and

"accessible" if I deposit it, it cannot help me if I do not do my part. Likewise, the grace of God is always accessible! Our "part" is simply to look to our Saviour in faith and ask for grace for our journey! Otherwise, we try to go on in our own strength, and we will be lacking what we need to overcome the enemy of bitterness.

As Paul continues, *"lest any root of bitterness springing up trouble you, and thereby many be defiled,"* did you notice that he says *"any root"*? That means it does not matter if the root is large or small. *"Any root"* that takes hold in our hearts and is not plucked out will trouble us, and it will also negatively affect those around us. Our lack of faith can cause us to have a pessimistic attitude and a sharp tongue. Bad attitudes, unfortunately, are contagious, and caustic speech will hurt those who love us most of all.

We see in Scripture and in life the danger of becoming bitter. We must guard against it in every way, beginning with *"looking diligently unto Jesus."* It is looking "on purpose"; it is looking with conscious effort. If our "eyes" from a spiritual perspective are not on our Saviour, we will be looking at the disheartening circumstances around us and the "flaws" around us will cause us to miss the beauty as we instead become bitter. It is so much better to look for the beauty!

Several years ago, I served the Lord as an evangelist. My family and I traveled across America conducting revival meetings and speaking in conferences; we did this for about fifteen years. One summer we were involved in church meetings on the gulf side of Florida. A man in one of the churches had a beach house on the gulf, and he kindly invited my family to swim and play in the ocean for an afternoon. We had such a wonderful time together! We had a cookout, played games, and went for a swim; how I cherish those memories!

At the time my youngest son John was about six years old. While we were in the water, John asked me to toss him up in the air so that he could dive into the water. We played together like this for awhile, and John loved it!

After several of these "dives," however, he went a little deeper and came up with a mouthful of ocean water! He immediately began spewing the water out of his mouth and with a tone of disgust he told me, "Dad, the water 'tasetes' like salt!" I was amused as I responded, "Yes, John, the ocean has salt in it." I held him in my arms as my frustrated son continued to spit out the nasty water. He then asked me, "Who in the world would put salt in the ocean?" I patiently answered, "Son, God put the salt in the ocean," to which John, in his six-year-old wisdom, replied, "It 'tasetes' terrible Dad, it's just terrible."

Of course, John was absolutely correct about the taste of the ocean water—it does taste terrible! It has a very bitter taste that unpleasantly lingers until you thoroughly rinse it out; but have you ever seen the beauty of the ocean?

My family and I sat that evening and watched the breathtaking sunset; the parade of colors— red, yellow, orange—was delightful to see. Then the sun seemed to slip into the ocean. It was such a beautiful sight!

I was reminded of all this several years ago when my wife Debbie and I went on a cruise. As we sat on the deck together in the evenings, we never tired of watching the sunsets. Early in the mornings I would return to the deck of the ship for my devotions and watch the sunrise on the ocean. I was again impressed by the power and beauty of God's creation. The ocean seemed to send the sun on its journey each morning and then meet it in the evening with welcoming arms. It was truly a display of beauty, majesty and harmony that only God could create!

Without argument, the ocean is one of the most beautiful sights in God's creation, but its waters are bitter! I was glad that my son John did not let the bitter taste of the ocean water spoil his enjoyment and his appreciation of the ocean's beauty. Within a few moments I heard, "Dad, I want to dive again, throw me up real high this time!"

My friend, life is beautiful! God shines upon our lives with His mercy, grace and love. Life is spectacular, and the Lord intended for you and me to behold it with wonder, joy and amazement.

However, there will also be bitter experiences that come into our lives—sometimes the cup of bitterness seems to virtually force itself upon us. Job said to his wife as he held his own cup of bitterness, *"shall we receive good at the hand of God, and shall we not receive evil?"*

When the cup of bitterness is forced upon you, when you dive into life and find a bitter taste, I want to encourage you from   Scripture to keep *"Looking unto Jesus...Looking diligently lest any man fail of the grace of God; lest any root of bitterness springing up trouble you, and thereby many be defiled...."*

God bless you! Look for the beauty of life along your journey!

Hope for Hurting Hearts Journal

Day 8: Look for the Beauty

Date:_____

Today's Scripture: Psalm 95

"My friend, life is beautiful! God shines upon our lives with His mercy, grace and love. Life is spectacular, and the Lord intended for you and me to behold it with wonder, joy and amazement."

*From today's reading I learned:*_____

_____

_____

_____

_____

_____

*On my heart today:*_____

_____

_____

~ Day 9 ~

What I Believed In The Dark

As you have read and journaled through the first eight days of this book, perhaps you have wondered if Don Woodard actually believes what he has written, or if he has ever had those beliefs put to the test. Dear Reader, not only do I have confidence in the truths I am sharing, but also I can tell you emphatically that what I believed in the light, I still believed in the dark. In fact, not only did I continue to believe the principles I am about to share, but they sustained me in my hour of darkness!

A few years ago my family and I found ourselves on a journey through the valley of the shadow of death when our daughter gave birth to our stillborn grandson, Caleb. Our hearts were crushed. We had anticipated a time of rejoicing, not a time of sorrow. As many of our friends heard of our loss, they called to offer their kind condolences, which meant so much. By this time an earlier book of mine, *When the Will of God is a Bitter Cup*, had been in print for about two or three years. A couple of close friends asked me a sincere question—with the right spirit. They inquired, "Do you still believe everything you wrote in your book?" I did not need time to think about how to answer this question; I simply and honestly replied, "With all my heart and then some."

The valley you are facing right now may seem very dark, but it is important for you to grasp this truth: what you believe in your heart—in your innermost self—will either help you or hinder you on this difficult journey. Every truth you have believed in the light, when life was bright and filled with blessings, you must continue to believe when the darkness has closed in around you.

When my friends asked me if I still believed everything I had written in my book, I began to see how important those beliefs would be for my family and me as together we walked through some very dark days. This realization prompted me to take inventory of what I believed "in the dark"; as a result, I found that my heart was strengthened as I prepared to preach my grandson's funeral service and as I reached out to minister to my family.

It is my prayer that, as I share these beliefs with you, you will find strength in your valley of darkness, just as the Old Testament prophet Isaiah wrote so long ago: *"Who is among you that feareth the LORD, that obeyeth the voice of his servant, that walketh in darkness, and hath no light? let him trust in the name of the LORD, and stay upon his God"* (Isaiah 50:10).

1. In the light I believed the Word of God, the Bible! I believed it was inspired by God and that it was perfect—without error. I believed it to be the eternal source of strength, wisdom and hope, and that it was sufficient for my needs! In the light I believed the Bible was the closest thing to Jesus Christ that I could touch and hold in my hands, and as I faced my hour of darkness, I still believed this was true. I still believed the Word of God!

2. In the light I believed that God loved me and that He loved my family. As we walked through this sad time, God was such a comfort to us! We were reminded of His love as we spent time in His Word and allowed it to minister to our hearts. We felt God's love as friends and family members verbally expressed His love to us and demonstrated that love through deeds of kindness. We received comfort through the great Comforter Himself, the Holy Spirit! In my hour of darkness I believed God loved me, and I believed it with as much conviction as I had believed it in the light!

3. In the light I believed that God had a perfect plan for my life and for the lives of my loved ones. I believed that everything happens for an eternal purpose, and that God is aware

of everything that transpires in His creation—even the falling of a sparrow to the ground. When I held my grandson's little casket in my arms, I still believed God had a plan.

4. In the light I believed that my Heavenly Father makes no mistakes—that nothing occurs without His knowledge and that nothing happens in my life without His permission. In my hour of darkness, I still believed that God makes no mistakes, and I knew I could trust Him even when I did not understand.

5. In the light I believed that God was always present and always near. In the hour of darkness, I knew He was still there, right beside me. When I was in high school, during one of the last weeks of each school year we had "final exams"; the students often referred to it as "the *big* test time." We would enter the classroom and sit down. Once class had begun, no one was permitted to speak; there was complete silence. The dreaded test would be lying on the desk in front of us, and soon the teacher would look at the clock and say, "Begin." As we worked on the test, he did not speak. Once the allotted time for the test had passed, the teacher would say,

"Put your pencils down and turn your test over." Now I knew that all the while I was taking that test, the teacher was present; occasionally he might even brush by my desk while I worked. I could not always *see* him during the time of testing, but I knew he was there.

Just as the teacher was in the classroom during that exam, whether I saw him or not, so God is with His children when they are confronted by the "big tests" of life. The psalmist David stated, *"Yea, though I walk through the valley of the shadow of death, I will fear no evil: for thou art with me; thy rod and thy staff, they comfort me"* (Psalm 23:4). Notice that David did not say "the valley of death," but *"the valley of the shadow of death."* Such a shadow, in our minds, is very dark and ominous; however, consider this: for a shadow to be present, there must also be a source of light somewhere! Light is always on the other side of the shadow. Although you and I may experience a time of testing that casts a shadow of sorrow over our lives, God is still there!

I believed God was present in the light, and I also knew He was present during the darkest hour of our valley.

6. In the light I believed in prayer. I believed God heard me when I spoke to Him, and that He wanted me to bring my burdens to Him in prayer. In the darkness, I still prayed! I prayed because, in spite of my darkness, I believed He heard my prayers. I did not have to understand before I could pray; I did not have to agree with my circumstances in order to pray. I simply needed to come before my Heavenly Father and tell Him all that was on my heart.

7. In the light I believed that God's grace was sufficient and abundant. In our valley of darkness we found that His grace was greater than our sorrow and greater than our pain. God's grace—His unmerited favor—brought us through our time of darkness. It was truly "marvelous grace"!

8. In the light I believed Jesus Christ was the Healer of the brokenhearted. In our time of darkness, I still believed He could mend the broken hearts of my daughter and son-in-law and the rest of our family, and He did not disappoint us. He remained true to His Word.

Everything I believed in the light when life was good and my soul was rejoicing gave me strength in the hour of darkness.

My friend, I do not know the specifics of your valley of darkness, but I want to encourage you to believe in the "dark" that God has not forgotten you, forsaken you, or failed you. His Word is still true, He still loves you, He is with you wherever you may be, and He has a plan for your life. God will hear your prayers, His grace is sufficient, and He will, in His time, bring healing to your broken heart. One day the sun will emerge from the shadows, shining its warm and brilliant light over your pathway.

God bless you as you journey toward that sunrise!

Hope for Hurting Hearts Journal

Day 9: What I Believed in the Dark

Date:_____

Today's Scripture: Psalm 143

".. . what you believe in your heart—in your innermost self—will either help you or hinder you on this difficult journey. Every truth you have believed in the light, when life was bright and filled with blessings, you must continue to believe when the darkness has closed in around you."

*From today's reading I learned:*_____

_____

_____

_____

_____

*On my heart today:*_____

~ Day 10 ~

When You and God Disagree

What a blessing it is to enjoy the company of someone with whom we share sweet fellowship and agreement! The prophet Amos, under the inspiration of the Holy Spirit, asked the question, *"Can two walk together, except they be agreed?"* (Amos 3:3.) On the other hand, the road we travel with that person becomes a little rough—or perhaps in our opinions impassable—when disagreement occurs. What is true of human companionships and relationships is also true of our walk with God; sometimes we will not see "eye to eye."

In I Thessalonians 5:18, we read *"In everything give thanks: for this is the will of God in Christ Jesus concerning you."* It is not an easy thing to give thanks in times of adversity, because in all honesty, we may not agree with what God has permitted to occur. What are we to do in times such as these? What do we do when we disagree with God?

In my own life I can say that God has been very good to me; I have seen many dreams fulfilled, and I feel that God has blessed me beyond measure. However, I am not saying that my life has not had its share of disappointments.

Not everything has worked out the way I had hoped; I have not necessarily been overjoyed with many situations. There have been times that I have disagreed with God in allowing certain events to take place, whether it was in the life of a family member, friend, or in my own life. I have had my heart broken more than once, and I have suffered the loss of people I cherished dearly. I have spent time in the valley of the shadow of death, and I have visited the cemetery. At these and other times I have seriously disagreed with God in allowing such heart-rending events to take place.

It is that way for all of us. Although it seems that some people suffer bigger heartaches than others, the truth is, regardless of the comparative "size" of the difficulty, we all share the general inability to understand what God is doing. We are unable to see our world from His all-knowing point of view; consequently, our human nature resists what God has permitted, and we disagree with Him.

The danger lies not in the disagreement itself, but rather in the potential for the discord to build a wall between us and God; for although we can never cease to be His child after being saved, we can certainly cease to delight in His presence! At this point, you may ask, "When I disagree with God, how do I avoid such a dangerous pitfall? What should I do? How do I move forward with my life?" Here are a few basic biblical principles to keep in mind.

1. When we face a situation in which we disagree with God, we must remember that **God knows more than we know, and He is always right!** "As for God, his way is perfect" (Psalm 18:30a). God is right in every decision He makes and in everything He does—whether or not we agree, approve, or understand. The Lord never makes a wrong decision, no matter how it may impact our lives; unlike frail man, He is too wise to make a mistake! Our amazing God, the One Who crafted the whirling spheres and brilliant stars in the heavens and Who designed the complexities of the human body is the same God Who is at work in the lives of His children. Nothing takes Him by surprise or suddenly "occurs" to Him as an afterthought. He makes no errors in judgment; He is always and absolutely *right*.

2. When you and I disagree with God, we must realize that **He sees much more than we can see**—He knows everything that is happening at this present time, but He also sees from eternity past to eternity future. In addition, our Heavenly Father is working in the lives of other people at the same time that He is working in yours and mine. Thus

God sees not only our situations, but He is also very aware of what is happening in the lives of people who are somehow connected to us, or who will be in the future. How many times would you and I walk through our valleys more cheerfully and with greater faith, if we knew that it would lead to a co-worker trusting Christ as Saviour, or a grandson surrendering to preach, or a brother in Christ facing his own trial with more certainty? The life of the Christian, like the life of our Saviour, is a life with "others" in mind, and times of trials and adversity are no exception.

3. When we disagree with God, we need to keep in mind that **our loving God wants the best for us, even more than we desire it for ourselves**. Now that may be difficult to accept when we are suffering, but it is nevertheless true. God does love us and His intention is never to cause us harm. The obvious reason why this life is not perfect is that we live in a sin-cursed world; but beyond that, God uses everything that takes place in our lives, whether it is a time of blessing or a season of sorrow, to make us more like Christ—to *"conform us to the image of his son"* (Romans 8:29). God wants us to trust Him, to have a close relationship with Him, and to lean on Him when life is

hard. Through salvation we become His sons, and as such we need to trust our Heavenly Father!

Remember that we are not only sons; we are also to be soldiers in this world. There are battles to be fought—battles for the futures of our children and for the furtherance of the Gospel! *"Thou therefore endure hardness as a good soldier of Jesus Christ"* (I Timothy 2:2). We can believe with confidence that our God will use all that comes our way to accomplish His will in our lives if we are yielded to Him! *"Being confident of this very thing, that he which hath begun a good work in you will perform it unto the day of Jesus Christ"* (Philippians 1:6).

4. When we disagree with God, we need to remember that **God has already done more for us than we could ever have done for ourselves**—and far more than we deserve! What you and I deserved was to be alienated from God forever in a terrible place called Hell. That "death" was the wages of our sin, not just the wages of Adam's sin in the garden, but the wages of our own sin! We deserved to be punished, because we were not only sinners because of our sin nature, but we also became sinners because we chose to sin! Yet God in

His love and mercy sent an unbelievable gift to mankind: He gave His only begotten Son to purchase our redemption by shedding His blood on the cross. Through faith in the Lord Jesus Christ, we have the promise of eternal life in the future, along with the ability to enjoy a wonderful life now as we are surrendered to His will.

I cannot speak for you, but I know that I have already received more from my relationship with God than I could ever hope to repay, even if I had a thousand years to serve Him! Consequently, I can come to terms with events in life with which I do not agree. The blessings I have received thus far in my journey have been gifts; I am totally unworthy of all God has done for me. In addition, I realize that the sadness I experience here in this life will be far outweighed by all that God has promised for me in Heaven, where I will enjoy the presence of my Saviour for all of eternity! The Apostle Paul phrased it like this: *"...Eye hath not seen, nor ear heard, neither have entered into the heart of man, the things which God hath prepared for them that love him"* (I Corinthians 2:9).

My friend, we will not always agree with one another, even in the closest of families, and we will not always agree with God, either. However, if we can just continue trusting Him whether we agree or not, we will one day be so very glad that we did. Surely if we can trust Him with our souls that will live forever, we can also trust Him with the "vapor" that is our lives here on earth!

God bless you, my friend, as you continue your journey.

Hope for Hurting Hearts Journal

Day 10: When You and God Disagree

Date:_____

Today's Scripture: Psalm 141

"Our amazing God, the One Who crafted
the whirling spheres and brilliant stars
in the heavens and Who designed the
complexities of the human body is the
same God Who is at work in the lives of
His children. Nothing takes Him by
surprise or suddenly 'occurs' to Him as
an afterthought. He makes no errors in
judgment; He is always and absolutely
right."

*From today's reading I learned:*_____

_____

_____

_____

_____

_____

On my heart today:

~ Day 11 ~

Singing at Midnight

It may seem that the topic of music has no place in our journey from hurting to healing, but for the Christian, having a song in our hearts throughout our lives makes such a difference! In times of joy, songs of praise to our Saviour flow from our lips as naturally as our next breath; yet the Bible offers examples of God's servants lifting their voices in song even in moments of despair.

When David wrote the following words in Psalm 57, we believe he was in hiding. Although God had promised the youngest son of Jesse that he would be king of Israel, the promise had not yet been fulfilled, and King Saul wanted David dead. Nevertheless, from the dreariness of the dark cave of Adullam, David offered a song of faith to his Heavenly Father. I have included below verses 1-3, as well as verses 5 and 9; interspersed among these David also poured out his heart to God as to the danger he was facing. Notice however, that the psalmist still offered praise to the Lord as well as confidence that God would deliver him.

> 1) *Be merciful unto me, O God, be merciful unto me: for my soul trusteth in thee: yea, in the shadow of thy wings*

*willI make my refuge until these
calamities be overpast.
2) I will cry unto God most high; unto
God that performeth all things for me.
3) He shall send from heaven, and save
me from the reproach of him that would
swallow me up. Selah. God shall send
forth his mercy and his truth.
5) Be thou exalted, O God, above the
heavens; let thy glory be above all the
earth.
9) I will praise thee, O Lord, among the
people: I will sing unto thee among the
nations.*

The book of Psalms is especially soothing to
the soul; not only have we included verses from
the book of Psalms in the journal portion of this
book, but we also encourage you to read at least a
few verses from that part of Scripture each day.
The word "psalm" in the Bible refers to a song,
specifically one that was accompanied by a harp.
Today we would think of a psalm as a sacred song
of praise to God.

In addition to reading in the book of Psalms
and meditating on its comforting truths, it is also
uplifting to read the compelling stories behind
some of our most beloved Christian hymns. Many
powerful, stirring songs were penned in times of
hardship or sorrow in the lives of the writers; the

messages of those hymns continue to minister to our hearts today.

Horatio Gates Spafford, a successful attorney, wrote the well-known lyrics of the hymn "It Is Well With My Soul" after suffering several traumatic events in his life. The first occurred in 1870, when his only son died from scarlet fever at the age of four. In the spring of 1871, Mr. Spafford began investing in real estate in Chicago, a city that was rapidly expanding; however, in October of that same year, he lost most of those investments as a result of the devastating Chicago fire. In 1873, Mrs. Spafford and their four daughters boarded a steamship for Europe, where they intended to have some relaxing time together as a family, away from the tragedies that had clouded their lives. Her husband planned to join them after finishing some last-minute business that required his attention. Sadly, their plans and their lives were drastically changed when the ship, struck by a Scottish vessel, sank into the cold Atlantic waters. Mrs. Spafford sent a solemn telegram to her husband that read, "Saved alone."

Mr. Spafford traveled to meet his grieving wife in Europe, and as his ship passed near the area where his precious daughters had died, he was inspired to write these words:

> When peace like a river, attendeth my way,
> When sorrows like sea billows roll;

Whatever my lot, Thou hast taught me to say,
It is well; it is well, with my soul.

Just as hymns such as this one touch our hearts, especially in our times of struggle, so I believe they also helped the writers in their own journeys to healing. Songs that lift up the name of our God will always bring comfort to the hearts of His children!

In Acts 16:22-34, we read about Paul and Silas, who were faithfully preaching about our loving God and His plan of salvation for mankind through the Lord Jesus Christ. In return for their compassion for the people of Philippi, Paul and Silas found themselves in serious trouble. Of what had they been guilty, apart from sharing the Gospel? While ministering to the people of this city, the preachers were confronted by a woman possessed by a demon, and they cast the evil spirit out of her. She was gloriously set free by the power of God! Her behavior while she had been possessed including "soothsaying" (we might call it fortune telling), through which some of the wicked men of the city had filled their pockets with money; so it was clearly greed and resentment that caused these men to drag Paul and Silas before the authorities and accuse them of being troublemakers.

After a brief trial the magistrates *"laid many stripes"* on Paul and Silas and then *"thrust them into the inner prison, and made their feet fast in the stocks."* This *"inner prison"* was a terrible place; to picture it in our minds we would need to think of a dungeon—dark and dismal, the little available air heavy with dampness and the offensive odor of filthy prisoners. There was no way to escape from such a place, for there was no window and only one door, which would be locked and guarded. Yet in keeping with the cruelty of Rome, Paul and Silas also had their legs fastened in stocks, certainly more to inflict pain than to keep them from escaping.

It is in these awful surroundings that we find two faithful servants of the Lord, beaten and bruised. No doubt they had not eaten for some time, so they also experienced hunger. Certainly their situation, humanly speaking, appeared as hopeless as it was unjust.

Most of us have never been in such a horrible situation, at least not literally. However, perhaps emotionally we have felt that we were in a dark dungeon, emotionally bruised and perhaps our spirits broken. Maybe that is where you are today.

I have often thought about Paul and Silas as they suddenly found themselves prisoners, treated with the sort of contempt that should have been reserved for murderers and thieves. I have wondered about their spirits as they began to grasp the reality of their terrible situation, and I have tried to imagine their mental, physical, and emotional suffering.

As though their circumstances were not already unbelievably difficult, it is also likely that they were subjected to the jeers of other prisoners—men who, unlike Paul and Silas, deserved to be there. Can you imagine the verbal attacks by both the prisoners and the Roman guards, harassing these men of God? Perhaps Paul and Silas heard sarcastic, cutting remarks such as these:

"Where is your kind and loving God now?"

"We heard you were preachers—what are you doing in prison?"

"Some God you have, letting you end up in this place!" "Your God must not be so loving after all! Does He even know where you are?"

"Did you come to preach to us?"

In my mind I can almost hear the laughter and the mocking. Surely these two men would have to be discouraged. Free to preach just hours before, they were now shackled together in that dark, dirty, and dreary place.

Scripture does not give us the details, so we can only imagine what was going through their minds. Perhaps Paul began to evaluate their dilemma and consider what their options were. Maybe he recalled his own actions before his conversion—he who had been a blasphemer of Christ and a persecutor of Christians.

In his physical pain Paul may have thought about the *"many stripes"* laid on him and Silas, but then he recalled how his Saviour had been scourged before going to the cross, suffering such anguish for the sins of the world, and for *Paul's* sins.

As Paul sat there, perhaps bleeding, he thought of how Jesus Christ had shed His innocent and precious blood on Calvary for Paul's redemption. There in that dungeon, that horrible pit, he may have also thought about how Christ had lifted him out of the pit of sin and had released his soul from the shackles of sin and Satan, to make him free!

Maybe as Paul considered his bruised and broken body and the sadness that tried to overwhelm him, he remembered that His Saviour had once mended his broken heart—and that this same Jesus Christ Whose Gospel he preached was still the great Healer of the brokenhearted.

There is no doubt that something began to well up within the hearts of Paul and his companion as they sat in this prison at midnight, for we read in Acts 16:25: *And at midnight Paul and Silas prayed, and sang praises unto God: and the prisoners heard them.*

I'm not sure how it all happened; I think God leaves some details to our imaginations. I can almost picture Paul whispering to Silas, "Silas, are you awake?" and Silas responding, "I am now!" The ensuing conversation would then have gone something like this: "Silas, let's pray!"

"What?"

"We need to pray."

Then after they had prayed awhile, Paul would say, "Let's sing, Silas! I want to sing now!"

"Paul, its midnight—and you want to sing? The other prisoners finally stopped yelling and went to sleep. You are asking for more trouble, my friend!"

"That is possible, Silas, but I want to sing. Let's sing and praise the Lord."

I wonder what the reaction was from the others in the prison that night. Somehow I think that singing to the Lord was something they probably had not heard there before!

I do not know the details of your circumstances; I can only conclude that you are reading these meditations because you desire encouragement and emotional healing. Perhaps you feel that you are in a dungeon and it is midnight. I encourage you to do what Paul and Silas did: pray and sing praises unto God. Do as David did while in the cave, *"Sing and give praise."*

My friend, through prayer we have the privilege not only of spending time with the Lord, but also telling Him about our burdens. In addition, both praise and good music can help to bring healing to a broken heart and comfort to a hurting soul; and what is more, offering praise to the Lord, even in our "dungeon days" will have an impact on the lives of others.

I encourage you to ask the Lord to give you a song today!

Sing and give praise to Him! You will find that a song in your heart will be a blessing; it will help to carry you through the toughest times of your life, and it will help you on your journey of healing.

God bless you, and remember to sing on your journey!

Hope for Hurting Hearts Journal

Day 11: Singing at Midnight

Date:_____

Today's Scripture: Psalm 57

"When peace like a river, attendeth my way, When sorrows like sea billows roll; Whatever my lot, Thou hast taught me to say, It is well; it is well, with my soul."

*From today's reading I learned:*_____

_____

_____

_____

_____

_____

*On my heart today:*_____

_____

_____

~ Day 12 ~

Mine Eyes Have Seen the Lord

My friend, what is your perception of God? While the word *perception* refers to how we view a person or idea, we all realize that we cannot literally "see" God; we do, however, have a "view" or basic understanding of just Who God is, and this will influence every part of our lives.

Whenever you and I are going through a challenge—whether it is a broken heart, a trial, or whatever words may best describe our circumstances—our perception of God is foundational to our healing, the renewing of our strength, and our victory. Without a healthy and biblical perception of God, life is hopeless and empty indeed! King David said in his Psalm of confidence, *"I had fainted, unless I had believed to see the goodness of the LORD in the land of the living"* (Psalm 27:13). Charles Haddon Spurgeon said of David's words, "Losing heart is a common infirmity, and even Goliath's slayer was subject to its attacks."

As I read King David's words in the above verse, it is as though David was in the valley of the shadow of death. He was burdened beyond description by his trials until he lifted his gaze from his circumstances to the Saviour. It was then that through the eyes of faith David "saw" the Lord, his "Shepherd" standing with rod and staff in hand, ready to rescue His lamb who was in distress, and to place him safely in the land of the living, and the land of hope, once again. The twenty-third Psalm describes David's perception of God as he had traveled this valley: *"I will fear no evil: for thou art with me; thy rod and thy staff they comfort me"* (Psalm 23:4b). The rod speaks of the long stick used to defend the sheep from predators, as well as to discipline the sheep when they were wayward; the staff, on the other hand, was used to gently but firmly guide the sheep, to draw them closer to the shepherd, or when a sheep had fallen, to deliver it from danger.

By faith, you and I also can find comfort in our Shepherd's "rod and staff"; the Lord cares enough to keep some harmful people and events out of our lives entirely and to discipline us when we wander from Him ("Prone to wander, Lord, I feel it"). He also uses His Word and circumstances to lovingly draw us closer to Him, to the point of lifting us in His arms if necessary and carrying us for part of the journey when we are too weary to take another step.

King David's words in Psalm 27, *"I had fainted* **unless I had believed**" reveal a great truth about hope, healing and the restoring process. The absence of faith will cause one to faint; without a staunch belief in God's mercy and grace, it is likely that we will give up altogether! Having a biblical perception of God is our best source of hope and strength, as well as perseverance through the trial. Such persevering leads to restoration and healing. Thus when we are in the valley of the shadow of death, we must "see," through the eyes of faith, the Lord Jesus Christ as the Great Shepherd, the comforting Healer and Restorer of our soul.

The Old Testament prophet Isaiah spoke of seeing the Lord in Isaiah 6:1-8:

1) *In the year that king Uzziah died I saw also the Lord sitting upon a throne, high and lifted up, and his train filled the temple.*
2) *Above it stood the seraphims: each one had six wings; with twain he covered his face, and with twain he covered his feet, and with twain he did fly.*
3) *And one cried unto another, and said, Holy, holy, holy, is the LORD of hosts: the whole earth is full of his glory.*
4) *And the posts of the door moved at the voice of him that cried, and the house was filled with smoke.*
5) *Then said I, Woe is me! for I am undone; because I am a man of unclean lips, and I dwell in the midst of a people of unclean lips: for mine eyes have seen the King, the LORD of hosts.*
6) *Then flew one of the seraphims unto me, having a live coal in his hand, which*

he had taken with the tongs from off the altar:

7) And he laid it upon my mouth, and said, Lo, this hath touched thy lips; and thine iniquity is taken away, and thy sin purged.

8) Also I heard the voice of the Lord, saying, Whom shall I send, and who will go for us? Then said I, Here am I; send me.

Through this vision given to him by the Lord, we see Isaiah's biblical perception of God. (Keep in mind that God used unusual means to manifest Himself until the time that the Scriptures were completed. There is no need today for God to appear to us in a vision.) First of all, it is significant that Isaiah introduced this passage with the words "It was in the year that King Uzziah died." According to many students of the Bible, Isaiah's ministry, primarily as a prophet to the nation of Judah, spanned from the latter part of Uzziah's reign until the days of Hezekiah. It is possible that Isaiah knew King Uzziah well as he began his ministry; we do know that Uzziah started out as a great king, but he finished poorly—going so far as to offer incense in the temple, which was forbidden to anyone but descendants of Aaron.

Because of his prideful action, Uzziah spent the last years of his life as a leper, and his son

Jotham became co-regent, reigning on behalf of his father then succeeding him after his death. No doubt the prophet Isaiah, the man of God for this hour in Judah's history, was saddened at the downward spiral of a good and godly king, and his death (probably from the natural course of leprosy) would have been very sobering. Our choices always have consequences!

Uzziah means "God is my strength"; he is also referred to in Scripture by the name Azariah, which means "God is my help." In the beginning of his reign, the king sought the Lord and did his best to do right in God's eyes. He knew that it was Jehovah Who was His true strength! God "prospered," or blessed him in this time of obedience. King Uzziah not only was victorious in his battles, but he also was successful in building up the city of Jerusalem, developing great armies, and even farming and raising livestock as a "hobby." He was reverenced by his people.

King Uzziah's death was no doubt a sad time for Judah, even though King Jotham had been the real authority for about a decade. They had looked to their beloved King Uzziah for hope and strength as they fought against their enemies; they had been proud of his many accomplishments, and they had learned to trust his leadership. He was their hero!

It was at this point in time, this time of loss, that Isaiah saw *"the LORD sitting upon a throne, high and lifted up...."* What an encouragement!

Even when earthly "heroes" fail us, our God never will! How wonderful it is to realize that even from our place of sorrow, from the valley of the shadow of death, we can "see" the Lord! Through reading His Word and spending time with Him in prayer, we can know that our Lord is near! No matter what our trouble or loss, God remains *"sitting upon a throne, high and lifted up...."*

Notice again the words of Isaiah in verses two through four.

> 2) *Above it* [God's throne] *stood the seraphims: each one had six wings; with twain he covered his face, and with twain he covered his feet, and with twain he did fly.*
> 3) *And one cried unto another, and said, Holy, holy, holy, is the LORD of hosts: the whole earth is full of his glory.*
> 4) *And the posts of the door moved at the voice of him that cried, and the house was filled with smoke.*

In this passage we see that Isaiah was keenly aware of God's holiness, His authority, and His unlimited power. In our own times of sorrow, we can look to God and through the eyes of faith we can see what Isaiah saw: our God is holy, He is the One true God Who reigns, and He is all-powerful. Looking to Him we can gain strength and hope—and we can renew our faith in His presence, His compassion and comfort, and also His grace.

A biblical view of God will reveal that He cares, just as a shepherd cares for his sheep; it will enable us to see that He is near, even when our situation is sad and sobering. A biblical view will enable us to see that God, unlike fallible man, is holy and His power has no limits.

There is something else that we can "see" when our perception of God is in agreement with Scripture: we can honestly see ourselves. What did Isaiah mean when, in response to seeing God, he cried out "W*oe is me! For I am undone*"? To be undone is to be brought to silence, to be destroyed or ruined; as he saw his true sinful condition before a righteous God, he knew that he had no wisdom, power, or ability of his own. He comprehended the danger of failing to depend on God at any point in his life, including in times of sorrow. He offered no excuses, he attempted no prideful boasting; he simply admitted his condition. Isaiah recognized his great need for God to work in his life if he was ever to do anything for the cause of righteousness.

Then Isaiah saw the angel bring a burning coal, taken from the altar of sacrifice, and place it upon his lips, which represented the purging away of sin, much like the refiner's fire would purge the dross from precious metals. Through this part of Isaiah's vision we see Christ's ultimate sacrifice for sin on Calvary; we also see His amazing love, and a picture of His continuing work in the lives of His children. Even God's servants sometimes need "purging"; we need the "dross" of this world removed from time to time so that we can be all that God intends for us to be.

Because our Lord experienced every heartache we could ever know, we can look to Him for strength, guidance, and hope. He is our Great Shepherd; may we take time to see Him sitting upon the throne, high and lifted up, and *able to do exceeding abundantly above all that we ask or think"* (Ephesians 3:20).

May God bless you, and may He be very real to you along your journey!

Hope for Hurting Hearts Journal

Day 12: Mine Eyes Have Seen the Lord

Date:_____

Today's Scripture: Psalm 27

> "...when we are in the valley of the shadow of death, we must 'see,' through the eyes of faith, the Lord Jesus Christ as the Great Shepherd, the comforting Healer and Restorer of our soul."

*From today's reading I learned:*_____

_____

_____

_____

_____

_____

*On my heart today:*_____

_____

_____

~ Day 13 ~

You Gave Your Best

"What more could have been done?" That is a question that can deeply trouble us when we are confronted by heartbreaking circumstances. We may never ask the question audibly, but within our hearts we are in turmoil because guilt shakes its finger of accusation and robs us of God's peace.

It usually takes a little time, but eventually questions of guilt surface in our minds, making our burden heavier still. We begin to ask ourselves questions such as these:

"Did I do all I could?"

"Did I do what was required of me?"

"Did I miss anything?"

"Did I do my best?"

And, then there is perhaps the most common question that causes the deepest emotional pain:

"Was there anything more I could have done?"

These questions and the emotions attached to them are normal for the grieving person, but there are some needed safeguards for us to keep in mind when feelings of guilt surface. By introduction to these principles, we will first read a passage from the sacred Scriptures, Mark 14:3-8:

3) *And being in Bethany in the house of Simon the leper, as he sat at meat, there came a woman having an alabaster box of ointment of spikenard very precious; and she brake the box, and poured it on his head.*

4) *And there were some that had indignation within themselves, and said, Why was this waste of the ointment made?*

5) *For it might have been sold for more than three hundred pence, and have been given to the poor. And they murmured against her.*

6) *And Jesus said, Let her alone; why trouble ye her? she hath wrought a good work on me.*

7) *For ye have the poor with you always, and whensoever ye will ye may do them good: but me ye have not always.*

8) *She hath done what she could: she is come aforehand to anoint my body to the burying.*

Mary of Bethany loved Jesus Christ and was a devoted follower from the time of her conversion. Although we have no certain evidence that she knew Christ would be turned over to the Roman soldiers and crucified—apart from His own prophesy concerning His death—we can conclude that the Holy Spirit led her to anoint her Saviour with the costly ointment. With a heart of love, Mary of Bethany came to Jesus Christ and anointed His head and feet; such anointing was customary in preparing a body for burial.

Some condemned Mary's gesture, but the one whom she ministered to said of her, *"She hath done what she could... Wheresoever this gospel shall be preached throughout the whole world, this also that she hath done shall be spoken of for a memorial of her"* (Mark 14:8-9). As I read those words, it seems clear that Jesus Christ was rebuking those who would have otherwise made Mary feel guilty, and He was assuring Mary that her demonstration of love was both noticed and sincerely appreciated.

Clearly, the Lord did not want Mary to deal with feelings of guilt, and that is true for you and me as well. Guilt will not help us through the heartaches and trials that we experience in this life. It is futile to reach back into the past and try to figure out if there was possibly something we missed—something else that could have resulted in a different outcome. Such mental exercises will only leave us more taxed emotionally, and they will hinder our journey of healing. So we must first of all come to terms with the fact that, at the time, we made the only decision or took the only action that we could, and we must **grasp the truth that guilt has no place in our healing process.**

Secondly, we usually need confirmation and assurance that we gave our best; we may even seek assurance from friends and family that we did all we could do—that we truly gave our all. There will always be those people who misunderstand our actions and intentions no matter how carefully we explain, but fortunately there will also be people in our lives who love and support us, and who give us the reassurance that we did all we could. It is important to **accept sincere words of reassurance and move on**, rather than to allow doubt and second-guessing to manipulate our lives so that we seem to ask again and again, "What more could I have done?" It is much like removing the skin from a wound before it has had sufficient time to heal, thus exposing it to possible infection, as well as causing repeated pain.

Once we understand that guilt hinders our healing, and that even those close to us are convinced there was nothing more we could have done in a particular situation, we must **be careful not to dwell on the negative**. To recognize that our action or decision was made with the best intentions is an important step, but it is just as important not to "replay the video" of what we perceive as the consequence of that action or decision. By this I do not mean that what has occurred to bring sorrow was necessarily our fault; perhaps it was something as painfully common as losing a loved one and not having the opportunity to say "goodbye." Guilt would chastise us for not being by that person's side, or even accuse us that if we had been there, our friend or relative would still be alive. Once we think that guilt has been effectively silenced, it can sneak back into the situation through negative thinking, which tends to replay the sad event over and over in our minds. There is no quick way to fix this problem; it requires diligent effort—staying close to our Saviour through Bible reading and prayer, remaining faithful to church services, listening to uplifting Christian music through the week, and also choosing to associate with fellow Christians who are excited about the future rather than stuck in the past. All of these will help us to avoid bitterness and, ultimately, depression.

Instead of dwelling on the questions of what more you could have done, focus your mind and emotions on what you did that was kind or helpful, or your best effort—and through God's strength, move into the present, trying to be alert to the needs of others around you and ways that you can assist them.

> Meditate on God's love for you, as well as on the love you have expressed to the dear people He has placed in your life; continue to demonstrate your love through kind words and deeds.

➢ Concentrate on the wonderful memories you have made and will continue to make in the days ahead.

➢ Focus your energy and effort on your own healing journey, as well as the healing of those who are on the journey with you.

➢ Direct your thoughts toward your current responsibilities and the people who need you now; they are depending on you!

➢ Refuse to dwell on circumstances and situations you cannot change; instead, turn them over to the Lord.

We can clearly see how we must not permit our lives to be weighed down with guilt, but rather take heart from the encouragement of others that we did our best. We also have to guard against thinking negatively on what is past, when there is nothing we can do to alter what has already happened. In addition to these three principles, it is important to keep in mind that **you and I cannot predict what the future will hold**; we can only look back. We have all probably told ourselves at one time or another how things could have been different if only we could have seen what was coming down the road. We sometimes even go so far as to predict how we would respond to some crisis in the future, but the truth is, we are only speculating! Until we see around the bend in the road—that is, until the situation occurs, we cannot know exactly how we will respond. This is a limitation that all human beings share, so we should not feel guilty for not knowing ahead of time what we might do, could do, or should do.

My friend, circumstances came into your life unannounced and you did what you could: you gave of yourself, you loved, and you did everything humanly possible. Do not allow pointless feelings of guilt to rob you of sweet memories and gestures of love that are rightfully yours.

Above all, **remember that God is not the author of guilt!** He knows more than any other being what our strengths, weaknesses, and limitations are, because He made us! In times of trial or tragedy, the Lord wants to be our Comforter and the Healer of our broken hearts. Remember, Christ is the "*author and finisher of our faith*"; it is through His gift of salvation that our faith had its beginning, and He will see that the work is completed. All the events that have transpired to this point in our lives, including the people involved and the very circumstances themselves, we must consciously place in the Lord's capable hands—and leave them there!

The Lord Jesus Christ told those who were critical of Mary of Bethany, *"Let her alone; why trouble ye her? She hath wrought a good work on me.*"

Determine by God's grace that you will not be burdened down with guilt; you have done what you could, you have wrought a good work. You gave it your best.

May God bless you as you continue your journey of healing!

Hope for Hurting Hearts Journal

Day 13: You Gave Your Best

Date:_____

Today's Scripture: Psalm 63

"Focus your energy and effort on your own healing journey, as well as the healing of those who are on the journey with you."

*From today's reading I learned:*_____

_____

_____

_____

_____

_____

_____

*On my heart today:*_____

_____

_____

~Day 14 ~

Choose When to Return

"I shall return!" This famous promise was given by General Douglas MacArthur when he was forced to leave the Philippines for a time during World War II; MacArthur followed through with his promise a little over two years later, and under his leadership the Philippine islands were freed from Japanese domination. Today we still remember those famous words he spoke during a very turbulent time in our nation's history.

My friend, we have been gently but consistently moving forward on our journey to healing. I pray that by now you can look back and see some victories God has given to you, as well as some areas of growth. Regardless of where you may be today, I think it may be time for "a roadside rest." Sometimes we need to find a spot to pull over and consult the "road map" of our lives—to see where we have been and where we are going. It may also be a time to reflect on a future decision—when to "return." In MacArthur's situation, returning represented deliverance of the Filipino people and a strategic victory for the Allies. For you and me, returning may be a positive and necessary step, or it may be one that draws us back into the shadows. In the latter instance, it would be wise not to "return" at all!

Most likely you are reading through this book because you have experienced the loss of a loved one or some other heartbreak in life. I ask that you be patient with me in this chapter because I have pondered carefully how to express the thoughts I wish to share with you. I want to be very careful not to say the wrong thing or make a hurtful statement. Also be patient as my introduction may seem lengthy, but I will arrive at an important destination.

We will begin with Luke's account of the resurrection of Jesus Christ, as recorded in Luke 24:1-12.

> 1) *Now upon the first day of the week, very early in the morning, they came unto the sepulchre, bringing the spices which they had prepared, and certain others with them.*
> 2) *And they found the stone rolled away from the sepulchre.*
> 3) *And they entered in, and found not the body of the Lord Jesus.*
> 4) *And it came to pass, as they were much perplexed thereabout, behold, two men stood by them in shining garments:*
> 5) *And as they were afraid, and bowed down their faces to the earth, they said unto them, Why seek ye the living among the dead?*

6) *He is not here, but is risen: remember how he spake unto you when he was yet in Galilee,*

7) *Saying, The Son of man must be delivered into the hands of sinful men, and be crucified, and the third day rise again.*

8) *And they remembered his words,*

9) *And returned from the sepulchre, and told all these things unto the eleven, and to all the rest.*

10) *It was Mary Magdalene, and Joanna, and Mary the mother of James, and other women that were with them, which told these things unto the apostles.*

11) *And their words seemed to them as idle tales, and they believed them not.*

12) *Then arose Peter, and ran unto the sepulchre; and stooping down, he beheld the linen clothes laid by themselves, and departed, wondering in himself at that which was come to pass.*

I draw your attention to the statement in verse six, *"He is not here, but is risen."*

During the approximately three and one-half years that comprised Christ's earthly ministry, He proclaimed that He was the Son of God, and He declared His purpose for being on earth: "to seek and to save that which was lost" (Luke 19:10). He walked among the people and healed the sick, the lame, and the blind. He cast out demons and raised the dead to life.

He also trained twelve chosen men to carry on His work. One of these men would deny knowing Him, while another would betray Him with a kiss—a symbol of friendship and loyalty—for a mere thirty pieces of silver! Then Jesus Christ was falsely accused, mocked, and spat upon. Hardened Roman soldiers beat His precious face with their fists and plucked out His beard. He was scourged with a cat-o'-nine tails, which was a leather whip with glass, bone, and metal fragments fastened to the ends of the nine strands. A crown of long, piercing thorns was placed on His head; then after these cruel acts of torture, they nailed our Saviour to a cross.

Think of it! The perfect Son of God experienced all this—and how did He respond? He prayed for those who crucified Him! Then when it seemed that things could not possibly be any worse, God the Father had to turn His back and look away from His only begotten Son, because the sin of the entire human race was placed upon Him. "For he hath made him to be sin for us, who knew no sin; that we might be made the righteousness of God in him" (II Corinthians 5:21). Christ died a death so physically and emotionally painful it is beyond our comprehension.

Our Saviour was buried and all was sadly silent for three days and nights—but then the Lord Jesus Christ arose from the dead! The tomb was empty! As the Scripture says, *"He is not here, but is risen."*

After Christ's resurrection, the only "return" that Scripture tells us about is His return to the ministry to which His Heavenly Father had called Him! He appeared and gave further instruction to the disciples before He ascended back to Heaven. Think with me now, because this is very important. There is no record of Jesus Christ returning to the grave, or of His walking back to Golgotha to see where His cross had stood. I also find it compelling that there is no record of our Lord reliving the emotions as Judas betrayed Him or as Peter denied that he knew Him. There is no record of Jesus Christ revisiting the time of His pain as He was scourged or when His Father turned away.

You see, my friend, there is a difference between **remembering** that you have gone through something tragic and daily **reliving** every event and emotion of the tragedy. Constantly revisiting the scene of our sorrow will result in deep depression! You and I cannot do anything about the fact that often we will remember difficult times as much as we do joyous ones, but we can choose not to rehearse the details over and over again! Choose not to "return" there!

Here is a place where I want to speak kindly and carefully, because I do not wish to sound unfeeling about your loss or heartache, but **there comes a point that we must rise up and leave our sorrow**. For forty days Jesus Christ lived near the place of His crucifixion and the grave where He was buried, but He did not go daily to relive it all. The point is, we cannot remain in the place of sorrow; we cannot remain in the "tomb" of continually reliving our heartache and the emotions attached to it.

There is a time to rise up and say of our circumstances, "I am no longer there, but I am risen." There must be a point where healing begins. Yes, no doubt some scars will remain; we will keep the memories, and there will remain a tender place in our hearts. However, **we cannot allow our loss or heartache to dominate the rest of our lives**! To do so is to choose a life of defeat.

There is a difference between living with something, and letting something be your entire life. Even today Jesus Christ lives with the reality that He was crucified and buried in a tomb. Throughout eternity He will bear the wounds that speak of Calvary; but He does not live today on the cross, and He does not live today in the tomb. *"He is not here, but is risen."* Jesus Christ is presently sitting at the right hand of God the

Father, and through His Holy Spirit, He abides in the heart of every believer.

My friend, whatever your heartache, trauma, or loss, you cannot remain there. Of course, I am not saying you should never remember the hurt you have experienced, or think of your loss, or that you should not visit the grave of a loved one. I am saying choose carefully *when* to return.

While working on this chapter, the Lord showed me something encouraging in Scripture that I wanted to share with you. On the day the Lord Jesus Christ's body was wrapped in linen and carefully laid in the tomb, the place of His burial was associated with death and sorrow; yet only three short days later that same location became a place of resurrection, life, and rejoicing. Even the very cross where Jesus Christ shed His blood and died is today a "place" of life and healing for every believer.

Someday your place of sorrow, trial, or difficulty could become a place of rejoicing not only for you, but also for others in your family. In the meantime, choose carefully when to return to the place of sorrow, but do not allow that past sadness to control your life. As I stated earlier, sometimes it is best never to go back to a place of hurt, because it causes far too much pain that we cannot seem to resolve; it is then that the Holy Spirit will wisely lead us to simply continue on with our lives.

There is one final thought I would like to share, because it affords so much joy and hope to the Christian. In John chapter fourteen, the Lord Jesus Christ was trying to help His disciples to be emotionally ready for His impending crucifixion and resurrection, but they did not understand His words at the time. There was a promise given to them that also applies to you and to me. Jesus said, *"I go to prepare a place for you. And if I go and prepare a place for you, I will come again, and receive you unto myself; that where I am, there ye may be also"* (John 14:2-3). One day our Saviour will **return** to take His children to be with Him forever! We will be reunited with loved ones who knew the Lord—what a grand reunion! And best of all, we will see our Saviour face to face. We will experience more joy than we could ever imagine, and the trials of this life will fade into insignificance. Paul wrote in Romans 8:18, *"For I reckon that the sufferings of this present time are not worthy to be compared with the glory which shall be revealed in us."*

God bless you and give you joy as you continue your journey!

Hope for Hurting Hearts Journal

Day 14: Choose When to Return

Date:_____

Today's Scripture: Psalm 116

". . . there is a difference between **remembering** that you have gone through something tragic and daily **reliving** every event and emotion of the tragedy."

*From today's reading I learned:*_____

_____

_____

_____

_____

_____

_____

*On my heart today:*_____

_____

_____

~ Day 15 ~

Conquering Life's Circumstances When You Cannot See the Purpose

Some time ago I was counseling with a very gracious lady whose husband had died of cancer in his early forties. Her husband was a pastor and together they had been serving in the ministry. During my conversation with her, she made a very powerful statement to me, one that sent me on a quest for understanding; she said, "The death of my husband would be easier to deal with, if I could just see the purpose." That is where most of us find ourselves when we are dealing with some heartbreaking occurrence. "What is the purpose of this in my life?" By searching for a purpose we seek to make some kind of sense out of a trying or tragic event. Mountain climbers talk about find a "foothold" or "handhold" that allows them to move forward with their ascent, and you and I desperately seek out a "foothold" of **purpose** that will enable us to move forward with our lives.

Unfortunately, we cannot always see the purpose of something God has allowed to happen. Perhaps that is what you are experiencing today. The "ascent" up the mountain appears treacherous, and there seems to be no foothold— just sheer rock. How can we conquer life's circumstances when we cannot see the purpose?

The word "purpose" refers to the intention for something, or the desired outcome or objective to be attained. Certainly our God is a God of purpose; all that He does and all that He allows has a purpose. Our lives have a purpose! God makes no mistakes, and within His domain there are no accidents. Everything God permits to enter into our lives has a reason. Sometimes the objective is to draw us closer to Him; other times it is for instruction, chastise-ment, or perhaps to bring us to our next level of spiritual maturity. God allows some events to take place in our lives for the benefit of others, and of course many things happen because we live in a sin-cursed world, and until such as a time as he is finally defeated forever, we have a wicked and powerful enemy. *"Be sober, be vigilant; because your adversary the devil, as a roaring lion, walketh about, seeking whom he may devour"* (I Peter 5:8).

Allow me to pause here and interject a very important point. It is not my place to tell you what God's specific purpose is for your life, nor to give a reason for your current circumstances. Instead, my goal is to give you encouragement—and I hope a little understanding—to help you on your journey of healing.

I will say that, based on the teaching of Scripture, the primary purpose for what occurs in our lives is that ultimately Christ will be glorified! All that God does is to point people to Jesus Christ, because God receives the most glory when people believe on His only begotten Son as their Saviour. It should help us to realize that whatever our circumstances are, God can be glorified through them and others can come to Christ for salvation. **God is able to take our worst circumstances and bring good from them.**

There are many verses in the Bible that are precious to me, but if I were to identify one as my "life verse," it would be Isaiah 61:3: *"To appoint unto them that mourn in Zion, to give unto them beauty for ashes, the oil of joy for mourning, the garment of praise for the spirit of heaviness; that they might be called the trees of righteousness, the planting of the LORD, (that) He might be glorified."* My friend, from your ashes God can bring forth beauty, from your mourning God can bring forth joy, and from your heaviness (heartache), God can bring forth praise!

As God works in our lives, it is our "job" as His children to trust Him, even when we cannot see the purpose of what He is doing; we call this faith! Faith is trusting God with our circumstances when we cannot see the reason for those circumstances. Faith is believing the Word of God and trusting in the promises of God, when we cannot begin to understand what God is doing! Faith is ultimately believing that God **does** have a purpose, although we may not realize what it is until we enter His Heaven!

Besides the necessity of faith, there is another important principle we need to grasp, even though it will not be easy. I believe that when you and I face difficult circumstances or heartache, God has chosen us to face those particular situations! Perhaps you would say, "How can that be possible? My heart is broken! How could God have chosen me for this?" Allow me to offer a couple illustrations from Scripture as well as the story of a special young man to hopefully help you understand this principle.

First of all, I do not believe that God *causes* bad things or heartbreaking events to happen in our lives, but based on Scripture I believe God *allows* things to happen. Our greatest example of this is Job. God asked Satan, *"Have you considered my servant Job?"* I am certain there were other men in that day who were spiritually strong, but God chose Job to be challenged by Satan. Think of Joseph in the Old Testament! Joseph was despised by his brothers, and they eventually sold him into slavery. Later he was falsely accused and placed in prison. After many years he was reunited with his brothers who had treated him so badly. Joseph said to his brothers, *"Fear not: for am I in the place of God? But as for you, ye thought evil against me; but God meant it unto good, to bring to pass, as it is this day, to save much people alive."*

God's Word does not reveal whether Job ever really understood the purpose of his trials, losses, and heartaches this side of Heaven; however, his testimony is extremely valuable, because it clearly teaches us that with faith in God and perseverance we can endure trials and heartaches in life. On the other hand, I believe Joseph lived to realize the purpose of his trials, in that God used him to save many lives—including his father, brothers, and their families—that otherwise would have been lost because of famine.

In addition to these examples from Scripture, I would like to share a touching story that also reveals God's choosing individuals for certain trials. It is an account that shows just how much our **perspective** can influence our attitude toward a situation. Several years ago I was preaching at a church in a southern state. The pastor and his wife, a precious young couple, had a little boy who was about six months old. This sweet little guy— whom I will call "Jimmy"—was born mentally and physically handicapped. His physical challenges included having no hands and no feet.

During the week I was with them, Jimmy was in the hospital. On Sunday afternoon the Pastor asked if I would be willing to visit his wife and their son Jimmy at the hospital, and of course I agreed to do so. As we pulled into the hospital parking lot the young pastor said to me, "Dr. Woodard, don't be alarmed when you see Jimmy. He is deformed and his appearance may be troubling to you." I simply replied that I understood.

When we arrived at the doorway of little Jimmy's room, the pastor greeted his wife with a kiss and a long comforting embrace. Then he went to Jimmy's bedside and just like any other daddy with a six-month-old son he began to talk to Jimmy in that language that only parents, children, and God understand. All the while little Jimmy was smiling at his dad, kicking his legs and waving his arms joyfully. It was a very precious and breathtaking sight to behold. Then I introduced myself to this happy little fellow. "Hello Jimmy. My name is Don Woodard. It is good to finally meet you—I've heard good things about you! You sure are a handsome young man." Although I was not Jimmy's parent, I like to believe that for those few moments God included me in understanding one of those special conversations with children. Jimmy's eyes wandered around the room as he once again waved his arms and legs with laughter. He seemed very happy that his mother and father were both there and that Daddy had brought a visitor.

My visit with Jimmy and his parents was an experience I will never forget; it caused me to pause and realize how blessed I am—and how small my problems were at the time. I also learned a very valuable life lesson from Jimmy's parents that day. As the pastor and I were leaving the hospital he said to me, "God has given me peace about Jimmy." He continued, "I realized that God chose me to be Jimmy's dad; I don't *have* to be Jimmy's dad—I *get* to be Jimmy's dad."

The pastor then went on to share with me about those first few days and weeks after Jimmy was born. There were other children in the hospital at that time who also had severe challenges. I cannot imagine how heartbreaking it would be as a parent to learn that your child has a serious medical condition, that he would be mentally challenged throughout his life, or that there was some physical condition that could not be corrected. Jimmy's dad told me that some of the parents had a tough time dealing with the stress of their child's infirmity and the uncertainty about what the future might hold; other parents just walked away, turning their children over to the hospital.

This young pastor and his wife may never discern this side of Heaven the purpose for their little boy's mental and physical limitations, but they came to trust in God's infinite wisdom, grace, mercy, and strength. They wore their heartache as a badge of honor because God had chosen them to be Jimmy's parents. They did not understand God's **purpose**, but they had the right **perspective**. It was a perspective of faith, and it gave them the "foothold" they needed to continue their journey.

The Apostle Paul, under the inspiration of the Holy Spirit, penned these words of comfort in Romans 8:28: ***"And we know*** *that all things work together for good to them that love God, to them who are the called according to His purpose."*

My friend, you may not see the purpose of your heartache now, but love God anyway. Trust Him anyway. Be assured in your heart that nothing has happened in your life without your Heavenly Father's knowledge. Believe that He has chosen you for something very special in His eternal plan—perhaps for you there is a greater glory.

God bless you! You are chosen for this journey!

Hope for Hurting Hearts Journal

Day 15: Conquering Life's Circumstances

When You Cannot See the Purpose

*Date:*_____

Today's Scripture: Psalm 10

> *"To appoint unto them that mourn in
> Zion, to give unto them beauty for ashes,
> the oil of joy for mourning, the garment of
> praise for the spirit of heaviness; that
> they might be called the trees of
> righteousness, the planting of the LORD,
> that He might be glorified."* Isaiah 61:3

*From today's reading I learned:*_____

_____

_____

_____

_____

_____

*On my heart today:*_____

~ Day 16 ~

Thorns that Remain

Have you ever been in a situation and felt like you were missing some strategic information? It was like a piece of the puzzle was gone, and without it the picture was incomplete. In the early days of my ministry, I can recall some experiences that made me reflect, "I don't remember anyone telling me about **this** in Bible College!"

Probably most of us have heard the following words of encouragement at some point in our lives: "God's grace is sufficient." That statement is absolutely true; in fact, it comes from a place in Scripture where the Lord Jesus Christ was encouraging the Apostle Paul. He said, *"My grace is sufficient for thee,"* and certainly you and I can draw strength and comfort from these compassionate words of our Saviour. However, there is more to the story than a statement about God's grace, and the Lord made sure we had the complete "picture" in His Word!

We find this account in II Corinthians 12:7-10:

> 7) *And lest I should be exalted above measure through the abundance of the revelations, there was given to me a thorn in the flesh, the messenger of*

*Satan to buffet me, lest I should be
exalted above measure.
8) For this thing I besought the Lord
thrice, that it might depart from me.
9) And he said unto me, My grace is
sufficient for thee: for my strength is
made perfect in weakness. Most
gladly therefore will I rather glory in
my infirmities, that the power of
Christ may rest upon me.
10) Therefore I take pleasure in
infirmities, in reproaches, in
necessities, in persecutions, in
distresses for Christ's sake: for when
I am weak, then am I strong.*

Let us examine this passage together carefully, because in it I believe we will find wisdom and practical help that we desperately need as we continue our journey of healing.

First of all, just what was the "thorn in the flesh" that we read about in verse seven? Some have surmised, based on clues from Paul's writings, that the thorn was poor eyesight, or even a terrible and rare eye disease. Others believe that the apostle suffered from arthritis or some other related illness that afflicted his body and affected his ability to do certain things, such as writing legibly. Certainly there is some evidence scattered through Paul's letters that make these speculations quite reasonable.

It is also possible that Paul's thorn was something emotional or spiritual in nature (of course, emotional problems *are* spiritual). After all, Paul also uses the descriptive phrase "the messenger of Satan" which was sent to "buffet" him. We know by the Apostle Paul's own testimony that prior to his conversion to Christianity, he was a very wicked man who committed terrible crimes against Christians and against the cause of Christ. Perhaps, then, "the messenger" referred to was a haunting collection of memories from his past life—a past that he could in no way alter. Keep in mind, however, that although Saul of Tarsus did not begin his life well, once he met the Saviour, Paul definitely finished well!

My friend, our enemy Satan would like to hinder our service for the Lord by using circumstances and people in our lives to continually remind us of past failures and sinful actions. At such times we must go to our knees and seek the Lord for His peace and strength to overcome these dangerous taunts. Our past before salvation is under the blood, and God will never bring them up to us again! And as His children, when we sin, we know that He will forgive us when we confess that sin to Him. *"If we confess our sins, he is faithful and just to forgive us our sins, and to cleanse us from all unrighteousness"* (I John 1:9). It is wrong of other people—even brothers and sisters in Christ—to bring up our past in order to somehow scold us or demean us. May you and I learn that lesson as well, so that we would not be guilty of inflicting this kind of pain!

Considering this list of possibilities, we must conclude that Scripture does not clearly and definitely state what Paul's "thorn in the flesh" was. That is good news for you and me, because we can rest assured that no matter what heartache, challenge, or valley we face, God's grace is sufficient for us!

Let's take a moment to look at the meanings of these two key words, "grace" and "sufficient." When we speak of God's grace, we are talking about His favor toward us that we could never earn—He bestows it simply because He loves us! *Webster's 1828 Dictionary of the English Language* gives a little fuller definition that I found very encouraging; that "grace" of our Lord also refers to His influence that brings renewal to our hearts and also keeps us from sinning against Him. What a blessing to know that when our hearts are broken, God will renew them because He so lovingly cares for His children! In addition, we can be confident that His grace is "sufficient"—it is graciously supplied in an "amount" equal to our need. God's grace is always enough! Again consulting *Webster's 1828 Dictionary*, we find that "sufficient" also means "qualified"! Think of it this way: friends may not have the strength or resources to help us—they may not be "qualified";

some so-called friends may forsake us altogether during a particular trial. In contrast, God's grace is always qualified to meet the need; in fact, it is really all that we need! Furthermore, God with His wonderful grace will never forsake us! Praise the Lord! Those truths bring hope and peace to the troubled heart!

Thus far we have seen that Paul dealt with some kind of serious difficulty in his life, but God gave him the grace to deal with it. Now as we look further, we find that missing "puzzle piece." The verse that states "My grace is sufficient for thee" goes on to say "for my strength is made perfect in weakness." God gave grace, but some "weakness" remained—because Paul's thorn remained! Paul wrote in verse eight that he had asked the Lord not merely once, but on three different occasions, to remove that thorn. Now I believe this was more than a brief request tagged onto the end of a prayer; Paul said he "besought" the Lord three times to take away his problem. That means he spent some serious time in prayer. It was not selfish for him to ask in this way, and it is not selfish for you and I to ask the Lord to deliver us from a trying or heartbreaking situation. We must realize, however, that sometimes—for whatever reasons our Heavenly Father may have—He may say, "No." Here in II Corinthians the Lord was telling Paul, "You are going to keep this thorn throughout the rest of your life, my child, but My favor toward you—My renewing of your heart—will meet your need and fill your void, no matter how much this thorn may trouble you."

My friend, if you have a loved one who has gone Home to Heaven, he or she will not return to you in this life, but God's grace will be sufficient for you, and even in this time of weakness God's strength will see you through. Perhaps you have someone who was dear to you just suddenly walk out of your life; that person may or may not come back to you, but God's grace will be sufficient, and He will strengthen you as you travel this difficult road.

Someone you are praying for may not recover from that illness, or you may lose your job even though you have asked God many times to allow you to keep it. The "thorn" may remain, but God is still good, He is still working to strengthen your heart and your faith, and He will walk with you every step of the way. He is gently saying to you now, "My grace is sufficient for thee: for my strength is made perfect in weakness."

Whatever your circumstances or heartache, you can put that situation in this statement: "My _____ may not be removed from my life, but God's grace is sufficient for me, for His strength is made perfect in weakness."

Paul continued with these words in verse nine, *"Most gladly therefore will I glory in my infirmities, that the power of Christ may rest upon me."* Paul "gloried" in his difficulty—that is, he recognized it was actually a blessing in disguise; the Lord used that trial to make his servant more like the Saviour. The Apostle Paul could have quit on God over this, or he could have become angry and bitter against the Lord for allowing it. Instead, he chose to accept the "thorn" as part of God's will for his life, and God no doubt used his life in an even greater way than He would have otherwise. Through trusting in God's sufficient grace, Paul brought honor to the name of the Lord Jesus Christ. He also encouraged others, including not only those in the church at Corinth, but also believers down through the ages who have read about his "thorn" that remained.

Remember the third verse of the hymn "Amazing Grace"?

"Through many dangers, toils and snares
I have already come,
'Tis grace has brought me safe thus far
And grace will lead me home."

These words written by John Newton during the 18th century have brought me great comfort and assurance over the years—the assurance of knowing that although some of life's thorns have not been removed from my life, God's grace will always lead me safely home! May you and I resolve, like the Apostle Paul, *"Most gladly therefore will I rather glory in my infirmities, that the power of Christ may rest upon me...for when I am weak, then am I strong."*

God bless you! Trust in His sufficient grace for your journey.

Hope for Hurting Hearts Journal

Day 16: Thorns that Remain

*Date:*_____

Today's Scripture: Psalm 35

> *"Through many dangers, toils and snares I have already come, 'Tis grace has brought me safe thus far And grace will lead me home."*

*From today's reading I learned:*_____

_____

_____

_____

_____

_____

*On my heart today:*_____

_____

_____

_____

_____

~ Day 17 ~

Who Is Bearing Your Burden?

Evangelist Bobby Roland, a friend of mine who is a cancer survivor, once said, "How much burden we bear ourselves depends on how much we give the Lord to bear for us." When you and I have heavy burdens such as grief and heartache, we feel like the weight of the entire world is resting upon our shoulders. That is the time we need to ask ourselves, "Who is bearing my burden?"

The book of Philippians is a book of joy and rejoicing, so it is no wonder that it sheds light on this idea of burden bearing. We read in Philippians 4:6-7:

> 6) *Be careful for nothing; but in everything by prayer and supplication with thanksgiving let your requests be made known unto God.*
> 7) *And the peace of God, which passeth all under-standing, shall keep your hearts and minds through Christ Jesus.*

Notice in verse six the words *"Be careful for nothing"*; the word *"careful"* literally means "full of care," or anxious. Our burdens bring anxiety! So God's Word instructs us not to worry, or be anxious, about anything. That sounds like a difficult request, but God does not ask anything of us that is not possible as we depend on Him!

The problem with worrying over a dilemma is that it accomplishes nothing productive in our lives; it keeps our minds preoccupied with what has occurred—or, more often, what **might** occur. You have probably heard it said that ninety-nine percent of what we worry about never happens! Worry can actually "paralyze" us in a sense from fulfilling even basic responsibilities, let alone trying to serve the Lord or reach out to others, because it becomes the main controlling factor in our lives. How sad to be sidelined, burdened down with care and anxiety, when God wants us to have an abundant life!

What, then, is the solution? We find it in the second half of that same verse: *"but in everything by prayer and supplication with thanksgiving let your requests be made known unto God."* The fact of the matter is, you and I will encounter situations that, humanly speaking, we cannot resolve. Through prayer we turn the entire matter over to the Lord, trusting Him to intervene on our behalf or to give us the wisdom and direction we need.

For those of us who like to accomplish a great deal on our "to do" lists each day, prayer itself may not seem all that productive, but that is not true! Prayer actively engages our Heavenly Father in our situation. Now He was already there, but you and I were too busy being "careful"—anxious, troubled, full of worry—to acknowledge His presence. Prayer helps us to focus on the spiritual aspects of our problem as we bring it to God, and all this requires effort. Ask any "prayer warrior" in your church, and he or she will tell you that real prayer is work!

> Prayer is trusting God with our sorrow, as we pour out our hearts before Him regarding our burden or heartache.

> Prayer is faith in action as we believe God **can** and **will** help us.

> Prayer is acknowledging the love and compassion God has for us, and that despite how bleak our world may appear, God truly desires the best for us.

> Prayer is consciously transferring our burdens onto the Lord Jesus Christ, knowing He is able to bear them far better than we ever could.

> Prayer is also interceding on behalf of others, even in the midst of our own heartbreak!

Did you take note of that fourth point in particular? When we bring our burdens to the Lord through prayer, it is not just to inform Him of our difficulty, or to discuss the details as we see them. Let me quickly add that even though the

Lord already knows what we are facing, He still wants us to tell Him about it! However, that is not the sole purpose of praying about the problem. The Lord wants us to literally "give" that burden to Him to bear! He knows our limitations, because He knows us better than we know ourselves; He realizes that especially when we are hurting, we are far too weak to carry the burdens of life. Besides all this, the more you and I trust the Lord to bear our burdens, the more our faith will grow.

The nineteenth century Irish poet Joseph Scriven faced much sorrow in his lifetime; nevertheless, he was able to live a life of helping others because he understood this principle of giving our burdens to the Lord. He wrote this poem in 1855, unaware that it would one day become a well-known and beloved hymn:

> "What a friend we have in Jesus,
> All our sins and griefs to bear!
> What a privilege to carry
> Everything to God in prayer!
> O what peace we often forfeit,
> O what needless pain we bear,
> All because we do not carry
> Everything to God in prayer!

Along with recognizing the importance of prayer, we also need to grasp the necessity of supplication: *"Be careful for nothing; but in everything by prayer **and supplication** with* *thanksgiving let your requests be made known unto God"* (Philippians 4:6). The word *"supplication"* has the idea of entrusting or pleading earnestly and with humility; so we are not merely to trust God with our burdens and ask for His help, but we are also to approach Him with an attitude of humility, acknowledging His greatness and our total dependence upon Him. We surrender to the Lord not just an isolated burden, but **ourselves** as well, in order that He might accomplish through our lives what He knows is best for us and for the cause of Christ.

Another key phrase in this verse is *"with thanksgiving."* Clearly, you and I should express gratitude for God's favor in our lives, and for the many mercies He has shown, but what about when we are confronted with a burden or trial? Is it possible to be thankful at such a time? The answer is a definite "Yes!" It may seem unreasonable to be thankful for what is hurting us, but we can have a spirit of gratefulness for a number of reasons.

> ➢ We can be thankful because **the Lord Jesus Christ Himself** has invited us to bring our burdens to Him.

> ➢ We can be thankful because we have a God we can absolutely trust with our burdens. He will never fail us, nor will

He ever misuse His knowledge of our burdens to hurt or betray us!

➤ We can be thankful because bearing our burdens is just one more way the Lord demonstrates His abiding love for us.

➤ We can be thankful because as we respond to our burdens as we are instructed in Philippians 4:6, we will have peace! *"And the peace of God, which passeth all understanding, shall keep your hearts and minds through Christ Jesus"* (Philippians 4:7).

In addition to this reassuring passage in Philippians, we also need to consider a "Great Invitation" recorded in Matthew 11:28-30; Jesus Himself spoke these words of comfort:

28) *Come unto me, all ye that labour and are heavy laden, and I will give you rest.*
29) *Take my yoke upon you, and learn of me; for I am meek and lowly in heart: and ye shall find rest unto your souls.*
30) *For my yoke is easy, and my burden is light.*

Notice that the latter two verses refer to a "yoke," which was a piece of timber used to keep a pair of oxen working side-by-side as they would bear a burden together. Christ said, "Take my yoke upon you" and also that His "burden" is light. Since Christ is bearing **our** burden (if we will give it to Him!) what is He referring to when He speaks of *His* burden and *His* yoke? There is really only one "burden" on Christ's heart today that He wants His children to share, and there is only one "work" that He would be speaking of, inviting us to join Him in His "yoke." As you and I surrender the cares of this life to the Lord, we are then free to be involved in something far more worthwhile that worrying! We can enjoy the "easy" yoke of serving the Lord—specifically, reaching this world with the Gospel of the Lord Jesus Christ. Through such means as witnessing, handing out gospel tracts, missions giving, and involvement in the various ministries of our local churches, we can work "side-by-side" with our Saviour! What a wonderful and amazing privilege! No wonder Christ says *"my burden is light"*!

There is one final verse I want to bring to your attention today, and that is I Peter 5:7: *"Casting all your care upon Him; for He careth for you."*

My friend, what burden are you struggling to carry on your own right now? I am sure that as time passes, it just seems to grow heavier and heavier. May I challenge you to take the Lord at His Word when He speaks of casting all your care on Him? Imagine for a moment that your cumbersome burden is tied up in a huge burlap sack. You have grown so weary of carrying this problem over the past several months—or possibly for many years now. In the quiet of this moment, why not place it at the feet of the Saviour? Tell the Lord you are tired of trying to carry it on your own, and that from this moment you are turning it over to Him! Yes, sometimes our human nature would have us take the burden back again, whether that troubling situation is related to finances, health, relationships, or other difficulties, but determine in your heart that you are going to follow the advice of this great song of our faith, which was written by Charles Tindley:

> If the world from you withhold of its silver and
> its gold,
> And you have to get along with meager fare,
> Just remember, in His Word, how He feeds the
> little bird—
> Take your burden to the Lord and leave it
> there.
>
> If your body suffers pain and your health you
> can't regain,
> And your soul is almost sinking in despair,
> Jesus knows the pain you feel, He can save
> and He can heal—
> Take your burden to the Lord and leave it
> there.
>
> When your enemies assail and your heart
> begins to fail,

Don't forget that God in Heaven answers
prayer;
He will make a way for you and will lead you
safely through—
Take your burden to the Lord and leave it
there.

When your youthful days are gone and old age
is stealing on,
And your body bends beneath the weight of
care;
He will never leave you then, He'll go with you
to the end—
Take your burden to the Lord and leave it
there.

Leave it there, leave it there,
Take your burden to the Lord and leave it
there;
If you trust and never doubt, He will surely
bring you out—
Take your burden to the Lord and leave it
there.

May God continue to bless you as you trust
Him with your burdens along your journey!

Hope for Hurting Hearts Journal

Day 17: Who is Bearing Your Burden?

Date:_____

Today's Scripture: Psalm 55

"How much burden we bear ourselves,
depends on how much we give the Lord
to bear for us."

*From today's reading I learned:*_____

_____

_____

_____

_____

_____

*On my heart today:*_____

_____

_____

_____

_____

~ Day 18 ~

Praying from the Cross

In our last chapter we noticed some key points about prayer as it relates to turning our burdens over to the Lord; today we will look at another facet of this subject. You and I recognize the value of prayer, no matter what our circumstances may be; however, when our hearts are broken, how should we approach God? And besides pouring our hearts out to Him, is there anything else we should do? In order to find answers to these questions, we will consider two events in the life of the Lord Jesus Christ, and also we will look closely at how He instructed His disciples to pray.

Before His crucifixion, Jesus and His disciples went to the Garden of Gethsemane for a time of prayer; however, His disciples were very weary, and not understanding that the Lord would soon be taken from them, they fell asleep. Scripture tells us that Jesus continued to pray earnestly. Since He was God as well as man, He knew exactly what was going to happen to Him. In a short while Judas would come and betray Him; Jesus would then be arrested, and His remaining disciples would flee in fear! He would then face the darkest hours of His life—alone. On the cross Christ would take upon Himself the sins of every person who had ever lived or ever would live in order for Him to *"taste death for every man"* (Hebrews 2:9), and in order to make a way for man to come to God. I believe our Lord took time to pray before these events took place for four specific reasons.

> ➤ The first reason was simply because prayer had always been a part of His life, and this hour of impending anguish was no exception. When you and I face terrible situations, it is not time for us to wring our hands in despair; it is time to pray!

> ➤ Secondly, as was true throughout His earthly ministry, Jesus was an example to us of how to live the Christian life; in order to live a victorious life as a child of God, prayer is absolutely essential!

> ➤ Equally important as the other two reasons is that the sinless, spotless Lamb of God desired communion with His Heavenly Father before He took our sins upon Himself and before His Father turned away because of that sin.

> ➤ Christ's prayer, forever recorded in Scripture, served another purpose: it unmistakably confirmed His total surrender to the Father's plan as He said, *"not my will, but thine, be done"* (Luke 22:42).

Also while in the garden, our Saviour prayed for those Who followed Him. This is an exciting truth, because Jesus prayed not only for His disciples, but also for those who would believe on Him in the future; in other words, His prayer included you and me!

Our second example from the life of our Saviour involves the first words He spoke from the cross. Again we see that He was praying as He said, *"Father forgive them; for they know not what they do"* (Luke 23:34). As you suffer through this time of difficulty in your life, I am sure you understand that it could never compare to the agony our Saviour endured on the cross; however, what you are facing is in a sense a "cross" that is causing you distress. (I need to interject here that when Scripture refers to taking up our "cross" it is referring to service for the Lord.) May you and I be challenged to follow Christ's example of praying from our "cross" of suffering, and to include praying for the needs of others as well as our own situation. **Often it is in reaching out beyond** **ourselves that we begin to find the healing we need.**

Earlier in Christ's ministry, His disciples had asked that He teach them how to pray; Scripture records this for us in two of the Gospels, including Luke 11:2-4:

2) *And he said unto them, When ye pray, say, Our Father which art in heaven,*

*Hallowed be thy name. Thy kingdom
come. Thy will be done, as in heaven, so
in earth.
3) Give us day by day our daily bread.
4) And forgive us our sins; for we also
forgive every one that is indebted to us.
And lead us not into temptation; but
deliver us from evil.*

As we consider how to approach God in prayer in
our times of sorrow or hardship, this passage
offers guidance through several important truths.

First of all, we must recognize to whom we are
praying. Jesus identified Him as *"Our Father
which art in Heaven."* If we have been born into
the family of God through faith in Christ, we have
a Heavenly Father, and you and I are His
children! When our hearts are broken or we are
facing trials, we can call out for help to the same
"Father" our Lord Jesus Christ called out to in His
hour of sorrow. What a blessing to know that just
as our earthly father used to pick us up and care
for us when we fell and skinned a knee, so our
Heavenly Father cares when we are hurting, and
He is ready to tenderly take us up in His arms
and care for our needs.

Not only is it necessary that we realize God is
our Heavenly Father, but we must also
understand that we are to approach Him with
reverence, as we see in those next words,
"Hallowed be thy name." He is God! He is holy

and righteous. There is no place in God's presence—even when we are hurting—for a flippant attitude that expects our every demand to be satisfied; we should not behave like spoiled children! We are to come to God in a spirit of worship, adoration, and submission. Yes, we are encouraged to *"come boldly"* (Hebrews 4:16) in that God wants us to bring our needs to Him, but we are still to enter our Father's throne room with respect; after all, He is the Creator and Sustainer of the entire universe!

We see next in this passage the phrase *"Thy kingdom come";* although this primarily refers to the future earthly reign of Jesus Christ, the word "kingdom" also has the meaning of dominion, authority or government. Even in regard to Christ's crucifixion, nothing took God or His authority by surprise! Calvary was our sovereign God's plan for man's redemption *"before the foundation of the world"* (I Peter 1:20). Of course, He did not cause Christ's suffering—it was our sin that did that—but God's righteous judgment was satisfied by His Son's willing sacrifice (Isaiah 53:11).

In our lives, although God does not cause bad things to happen, nor is it His desire that we suffer, God still has dominion as He permits certain events to occur; moreover, He can use our times of sorrow, pain, or other turmoil to accomplish potentially great things for our good and His glory! Thus God has dominion over every aspect of our lives—even our "crosses."

Notice that this verse also says, *"Thy will be done."* Even in our worst circumstances we should pray for God's will to be fulfilled. As we discussed earlier, that is how Jesus Christ prayed in the Garden of Gethsemane. In the garden as well as from the cross, Jesus Christ without reservation or hesitancy trusted God the Father. **I believe the truest form of worship is to trust God completely, even in the face of adversity.**

Thus far in these verses in Luke chapter 11, we have seen that we need to recognize to Whom we are praying, that we must come to God with reverence, and that even in our times of difficulty, we are to seek His will rather than our own. We notice fourthly that we should ask the Lord for what we need, and we do so for each day. Christ taught His disciples to ask of God, *"Give us day by day our daily bread."* In Scripture the word "bread" generally refers to physical nourishment for physical strength. In John 6:35, on the other hand, the "bread" that is described is of a spiritual nature; it speaks of knowing Christ as Saviour and having a relationship with Him. Jesus Christ said, *"I am the bread of life; he that cometh to me shall never hunger; and he that believeth on me shall never thirst."*

On our journey of healing, it is vital that we ask God for our daily spiritual sustenance—that is, for the spiritual and emotional wisdom and strength that we need to get through today. Much of that nourishment will come from reading the Word of God; as we pray about God's provision, He will give us understanding of what we read. The writer of Psalm 119 petitioned the Lord *"Open thou mine eyes, that I may behold wondrous things out of thy law."* In addition, as we talk to the Lord each day along our journey, He will give grace and strength for the day at hand. There is no need for God to provide for tomorrow's challenges today, and it is unwise for us to speculate and borrow from tomorrow's trouble!

Keep in mind also that healing for our hurting hearts is a day-by-day process. Just as it is not possible to take a single pill and suddenly be cured of a serious disease, so there is no "one-minute cure" for a broken heart! We must proceed through our journey step by step (and prayer by prayer); by faith we can be assured that we will reach our destination of healing.

All that we have learned from this passage about prayer during our time of sorrow has been very important, but we dare not miss this next point: forgive and be forgiven. *"And forgive us our sins; for we also forgive everyone that is indebted to us."* The Lord Jesus Christ had no sin to confess as He prayed from the cross. He was God clothed in humanity; He was and is perfectly sinless. You and I, however, are born with a sin nature; we are sinners by birth as well as by choice. Once we have trusted Christ as our

Saviour and been redeemed by grace through faith, our sins are forgiven and forgotten! However, if at some point we allow something great or small to come between us and our Heavenly Father, we need to deal with that issue. For example, if in the midst of our trials we have become angry or resentful, possibly blaming God for our pain, we need to confess that sin to Him, and He will forgive us. Also, if we have allowed someone's actions to cause us to harbor feelings of bitterness, strife, envy, or malice toward that person, not only do we need to ask the Lord to forgive us, but also we need to forgive the individual who, in our minds, wronged us in some way.

As a necessary part of our healing, we must forgive others, and as strange as it may sound, sometimes we need to forgive ourselves as well! Perhaps there was a decision that was made months, or even years ago; that decision, in our opinion, was the catalyst that led to financial difficulty or some other serious misfortune that could never be satisfactorily resolved. As members of the imperfect human race, our best option is to forgive ourselves, and then to turn the situation over to the Lord and move on with our lives.

Let God search your heart today. Confess to Him any wrong feelings you may be harboring against someone, then forgive that person. Forgive and be forgiven!

In addition to being quick to forgive others and to seek forgiveness for ourselves, we must always be on guard against temptation. By making this request of the Lord, *"Lead us not into temptation,"* we are in essence asking Him to help us to stay far away from situations in which we might be enticed to do anything that would bring dishonor to our Saviour.

When trials and tribulations come to us, so do temptations. We may be tempted to doubt God and His Word, or to lose faith in His love for us, or we may be tempted to become angry and bitter. We must pray from our "cross" and ask the Lord to help us so that we do not yield to these temptations.

In the last verse of our passage we read *"deliver us from evil."* There is an evil power in this world, and his name is Satan. He is not omnipresent like God, but he has demons that do his bidding. Our prayer when we are in a heartbreaking situation should be a prayer of being rescued from the evil influence of the *"prince of the power of the air, the spirit that now worketh in the children of disobedience"* (Ephesians 2:2). You see, while God can use even our most difficult trials to bring about good in our lives, Satan would like to see our sorrow oppress and destroy us! The enemy wants us to become angry and resentful toward God so that we eventually walk away from Him and go our own way (which is really Satan's way). It may seem that our pain or hardship will never end, but in the meantime God can deliver us from the kind of wicked influence that would cause us to walk away from the One Who gave His life for us.

My friend, the most important thing you will do today is pray from your "cross."

God bless you! Talk to God in prayer every day as you continue on your journey.

Hope for Hurting Hearts Journal

Day 18: Praying From the Cross

Date:_____

Today's Scripture: Psalm 22

"We must proceed through our journey
step by step (and prayer by prayer); by
faith we can be assured that we will
reach our destination of healing."

From today's reading I learned:_____

_____

_____

_____

_____

_____

On my heart today:_____

_____

_____

_____

~ Day 19 ~

When I Come Forth as Gold

Without question the most famous man in the history of suffering is Job; in fact, it is not uncommon to hear even someone with little knowledge of the Bible or Christianity refer to this man by name when talking about trials. When we think of people who have survived terrible heartache and overcome great obstacles, Job has earned a rightful place at the top of the list.

We discussed Job's trials at length in an earlier chapter (Day 2). Scripture records for us that Job received terrible news of devastating losses: his ten precious children, his employees, his wealth, his source of income—and all these tragic events occurred in less than one day's time! Shortly after this, he also lost his health; men who had been his friends came to console him, but ended up accusing him of sinning against God and thus bringing upon himself judgment from the Almighty. Despite all that happened to Job, he remained a man of great faith in the Lord, a man of faithful worship in good times or bad, and a man of hope as he looked toward the future. These strengths displayed by this Old Testament saint centuries ago are still important strengths today for anyone who is on this challenging journey of healing.

As we think about our topic today, "When I Come Forth As Gold," my desire is that after we examine some additional thoughts from Job's life, your future will look brighter to you. Like Job, you can reach the end of your journey and see that God has made your life even more valuable than it was before the trial or tragedy took place—not necessarily in earthly wealth, but maybe through your service for the Lord or your compassionate heart toward others who are hurting. I do not know the details of what will occur in your life, but I am convinced you can "come forth as gold"!

When questioned by one of his "friends" regarding his character and spiritual condition, Job's response included these words: "he knoweth the way that I take: when he hath tried me, I shall come forth as gold" (Job 23:10). What a powerful statement! It reveals Job's faith in the midst of his sorrow, as well as his hope for the future.

First of all, we see that **Job had faith that he could reach out to God in his time of need and be comforted.** He believed in his heart that in spite of his suffering, by faith he could stand in the very presence of His Lord and be receive the consolation he so desperately needed. My friend, sometimes our hurt is so deep that it is difficult to pray the simplest prayer; we may find ourselves in a situation that all we seem to be able to say is "God, please help!" Other times we may not be able to speak at all. Our only "prayer" is our tears, but God understands the message of our tears!

Let me reassure you that just as God's comfort was available to Job, it is also available to you! Through prayer (even the silent cry of your heart), and through reading and meditating on the Word of God, you can enter into the presence of God and *"find grace to help in time of need"* (Hebrews 4:16b). In addition, as a believer in Jesus Christ, you have the Holy Spirit dwelling within you, and He is the great Comforter.

Secondly, it is also evident that **Job had faith that God would give him the strength he needed to endure his tribulation.** In Job 23:6 Job said, *"Will he plead against me with his great power? No; but he will put strength in me."* Although Job was in the valley of suffering and heartache, he maintained confidence in God's strength, and he believed that God would empower him in this time that he felt so very weak. My friend, the same strength afforded Job can be yours today; it brings our Heavenly Father great pleasure to strengthen His children as we realize just how weak we are and how much we need Him! The prophet Isaiah penned the following words that have blessed countless people down through time: *"But they that wait upon the Lord shall renew their strength; they shall mount up with wings as eagles; they shall run, and not be weary; and they shall walk, and not faint"* (Isaiah 40:31).

Thirdly, **Job believed that God was there even though He could not be seen, and that He**

was actively involved in the life of His child, working toward a definite plan for Job's future.
"Behold, I go forward, but he is not there; and backward, but I cannot perceive him: On the left hand, where he doth work, but I cannot behold him: he hideth himself on the right hand, that I cannot see him" (Job 23:8-9). These thoughts directly precede the primary verse we are dealing with today: *"But* [in other words, the fact that Job could not see God was of no consequence!] *he knoweth the way that I take: when he hath tried me, I shall come forth as gold."* Clearly Job possessed hope, despite his trials—and regardless of the fact that God could be "seen" only through the eyes of faith!

When you and I can almost sense the cold surrounding us in our dark valley, we may not feel the warmth of God's presence. It is difficult to "see" the Saviour when our heart is filled with grief and our eyes are filled with tears! Nevertheless, just as the sun is still there even when it is hidden behind the dark clouds, so God is still there when we are in the midst of our trouble and we do not sense His presence. Though the dreary clouds of grief may block His warmth along with our view of Him, God is always there! Job's present hour was one of darkness, yet he still believed that God was near and that He had a plan for Job's life. This man's faith in the Lord produced hope that would carry Job through the valley. My friend, hope is something that you and

I must not lose. The Bible's use of the word "hope" does not mean some kind of empty wishful thinking; instead it is a desire for something that also has expectation or confidence that it will come to pass!

Look carefully again at Job's expression of hope: *"he* [God] *knoweth the way that I take: when he hath tried me, I shall come forth as gold."* Job knew in his heart that humanly speaking he was doing everything he could possibly do. He knew that his life, his future, and his healing rested in God alone, and that is where he placed his hope— not in his own abilities. That is good advice for us today!

Also notice the phrase, *"when he hath tried me"*; Job believed in his heart that God knew the details of his suffering, as well as all that had ever taken place in Job's life. His words reveal something else as well; despite Job's struggle with his great sorrow, he was nevertheless confident that ultimately God was the One Who was in control. He did not blame God for causing the pain from all his losses, but he realized that God had allowed all those events to take place. Job also recognized that God was concerned for him and all he was going through.

My friend, please do not lose sight of the following truths; I have made these statements before, but they definitely bear repeating. God does not make bad things happen to people. However, nothing occurs unless God permits it. At this moment you may feel that you have completely lost control of your circumstances, and that is not unusual when we have suffered a loss or we are facing a severe trial. The sense of order we enjoyed in our lives has been disrupted, and all that we knew as "normal" has suddenly and drastically changed. Continue to trust God as Job did, and believe that God has not lost control. You can also rest assured that God is concerned for you and your circumstances as much as He was for Job and his situation.

"I shall come forth as gold"; what a victorious statement! Look carefully at the entire verse again. *"But he knoweth the way that I take: when he hath tried me, I shall come forth as gold."* I can picture Job sitting in the ashes, his heart broken from all that he had lost, especially the death of his children. His burdens were made heavier by the accusations of his so-called friends, and as he scraped the painful, oozing boils from his flesh with the potsherd, I can almost see Job looking up toward heaven and declaring boldly to his friends, *"He knoweth the way that I take: when he hath tried me, I shall come forth as gold. My foot hath held his steps, His way have I kept, and not declined. Neither have I gone back from the commandment of his lips; I have esteemed the words of his mouth more than my necessary food."*

There was so much meaning behind those words that Job spoke!

- *"I shall come forth as gold."*
  <u>My present situation is not forever</u>; I believe that one day I will experience God's hand of blessing again.

  (Job had a right heart attitude about his circumstances. He had lost so much, but he had not lost his faith in God or his hope in the promises of God's Word.)

- *"I shall come forth as gold."*
  <u>I may be down now, but I am going to get back up.</u> I may be in the valley of sorrow, but I have set my gaze toward the mountaintop, and I am even now moving toward that mountain. At this moment I cannot see God because of the tears in my eyes and the grief in my heart, but I know God is there.

- *"I shall come forth as gold."*
  Just like gold that has been tried in the fire, <u>I will be stronger and I will shine brighter.</u> The dross will be removed from my life, and I will be purified. In God's time, I will be ready for Him to use me as He sees fit, to fulfill His purpose. In the meantime, His words will sustain me and strengthen me. In my present condition I surrender my life and my circumstances to the Master Goldsmith to form me as He pleases, and to make of my life that which will glorify Him the most.

My friend, from your circumstances, from your ashes, speak these words aloud to your own heart: *"He knoweth the way that I take: when he hath tried me, I shall come forth as gold."*

God bless you! May your faith and hope grow stronger, knowing one day on your journey you, too, will *"come forth as gold"*!

Hope for Hurting Hearts Journal

Day 19: When I Come Forth as Gold

Date:_____

Today's Scripture: Psalm 17

"Just like gold that has been tried in the
fire, I will be stronger and I will shine
brighter. The dross will be removed from
my life, and I will be purified. In God's
time, I will be ready for Him to use me
as He sees fit, to fulfill His purpose."

*From today's reading I learned:*_____

_____

_____

_____

_____

*On my heart today:*_____

_____

_____

_____

~ Day 20 ~

Encountering Change

Change is an inevitable part of life; sometimes it is a happy or even exciting event, while other times it is an unpleasant one. Either way, most of us tend to resist it, because we are comfortable with our circumstances the way they are! Some of the most trying and difficult types of change are ones which affect our personal lives, especially those that bring disappointment or heartbreak.

Some time ago I was privileged to meet with a young veteran who had served three tours of military duty: two in Iraq and one in Afghanistan. Our conversation turned into an impromptu counseling session as he began to share some of the challenges he was facing since returning to civilian life. At one point I asked him, "What is the most difficult thing about being home?"

"Change," he responded. "There is a different pace in war; it is a different environment, and everything is structured for you." I was surprised by that answer, but at the same time I appreciated his frankness; it helped me to better understand this situation that confronts many of our men and women in the military.

As we consider today's topic, "Encountering Change," our focus will be on Christ's disciples and some of the stressful changes they had to contend with. We will also make some practical applications that I believe will be helpful and encouraging to you on your journey.

Imagine with me the day-to-day lives of these twelve men who were chosen to be a part of Christ's earthly ministry. It was not long before the disciples realized that miracles were common occurrences wherever Jesus went! The lame could walk again, blind people were made to see, an only son was raised from the dead, a woman with an incurable illness was healed, and hundreds if not thousands of other astonishing events took place. "Thousands" may seem like an exaggeration until we recall the closing words found in the Gospel of John: *"And there are also many other things which Jesus did, the which, if they should be written every one, I suppose that even the world itself could not contain the books that should be written"* (John 21:25).

Besides being amazed by all the wonderful miracles, the disciples were also privileged to hear Christ teach; sometimes multitudes were present, other times it was just the Lord and them. Think what it must have been like to hear the One Who is the Living Word impart life-changing truth!

Certainly being one of the Lord's disciples was an enviable position in many respects, as they witnessed the supernatural and heard the voice of God's Son! Perhaps the greatest blessing these men received, however, was the love Jesus had for each of them, as well as the privilege to love Him in return and to be in His presence every day for those three and a half years! They ate with Him, lived as He lived, and observed both His divinity and His humanity.

Then came the day that change, like a powerful storm, destroyed the serenity of their world, leaving behind hearts that were broken and dreams that were shattered. Their lives were drastically altered as their kind and loving Master was suddenly taken away from them. One evening they had observed the Passover together, and the next day Jesus was crucified! The disciples were convinced that life would never be the same again. They were devastated.

Another follower of Christ, Joseph of Arimathaea, asked permission of Pontius Pilate to bury Jesus; Scripture gives us more information about the burial in John 19:38-42:

> 38) *And after this Joseph of Arimathaea, being a disciple of Jesus, but secretly for fear of the Jews, besought Pilate that he might take away the body of Jesus: and Pilate gave him leave. He came therefore, and took the body of Jesus.*
> 39) *And there came also Nicodemus, which at the first came to Jesus by night, and brought a mixture of myrrh and aloes, about an hundred pound weight.*

40) *Then took they the body of Jesus, and wound it in linen clothes with the spices, as the manner of the Jews is to bury.*
41) *Now in the place where he was crucified there was a garden; and in the garden a new sepulchre, wherein was never man yet laid.*
42) *There laid they Jesus therefore because of the Jews' preparation day; for the sepulchre was nigh at hand.*

Consider those first two days after Christ's death, and what it must have been like for the disciples as their minds continued to replay all that had occurred. The betrayal, the arrest, the crucifixion—and now Jesus' body lay in a tomb. There were no words that could adequately express the disciples' sense of loss. With these events behind them, perhaps they hoped that all the changes were over, but that was not the case. Notice what is recorded in John 21:1–2:

1) *The first day of the week cometh Mary Magdalene early, when it was yet dark, unto the sepulchre, and seeth the stone taken away from the sepulchre.*
2) *Then she runneth, and cometh to Simon Peter, and to the other disciple, whom Jesus loved, and saith unto them, They have taken away the Lord out of*

the sepulchre, and we know not where
they have laid him.

The disciples doubted her story, but when they reached the tomb, they saw for themselves that it was indeed empty! Of course they believed that His body had been stolen. They must have wondered why life had suddenly become so complicated and why their world had to be in a state of constant change. Even though Christ had tried to prepare His disciples by telling them what would occur, they had not understood. They had never anticipated anything like the events of the last few days. They felt unprepared in every way to handle it all.

The grey clouds of sorrow were replaced by brilliant sunlight when the disciples saw with their own eyes that Jesus was alive—He had risen from the dead! **This** change they encountered was a welcome one! The sadness and confusion of the prior days was gone; instead the disciples experienced overwhelming happiness and the dawning of understanding as to the Saviour's purpose in coming to this world. The changes were not over, but at least when Jesus told them He would be leaving, they understood; after forty days of once again enjoying His presence and listening carefully to His instructions, they watched as Christ ascended back to Heaven (Acts 1:9).

These faithful followers of the Lord continued to encounter change after Christ returned to His Heavenly Father. If they had not realized it before, they understood now that such change was an inevitable part of life. That is true for us as well, but take heart! The same Lord Who helped the disciples over every hurdle will help you and me with the changes and challenges of life.

Even though the disciples knew where Jesus was and also knew firsthand that He was alive, it was still very difficult to be separated from Him. He was Someone Who loved them very much and Whom they loved. He was their dearest Friend! Jesus represented comfort and security, as well as a love they could always count on. He had also been a teacher and mentor Who had instilled much godly wisdom in their hearts and minds.

As you and I encounter change in our lives that comes from the loss of someone dear, what can we do? In some cases, the loss is a friend or loved one who has crossed over from this life into eternity; in other instances the word "loss" does not begin to explain the hurt we feel inside because someone has just walked away! My friend, there is a precious Saviour Who loves you; He has already conquered death, and He is a Friend Who will never, under any circumstances, leave you. You can go directly to Him through prayer and find comfort for your hurting heart.

Besides reaching out to the Lord, we can also reach out to those who still bless our lives with their love, their ability to comfort us when our world is upside down, and the way they make us feel safe, whether it is safety in our surroundings or that we feel secure sharing anything with them. Hold these friends and loved ones close and let them know they are precious! Demonstrate that you will "be there" for them just as they have been for you.

In addition, we can strive to make a difference in the lives of others in our churches and communities who have never known what it means to be loved or to have a real friend. Involvement in our churches' bus ministries, Sunday school classes, as well as outreach into various neighborhoods will open our eyes to the great needs around us. Perhaps we can one day teach a group of children or mentor another adult. Maybe we can show the love of Christ by spending time with some elderly people in a nursing home; often these residents feel as though they have been abandoned and forgotten. While these suggestions will not remove all the hurt, as we invest in others and find our real security in the Lord, we will gradually find healing—and someone will be thanking God that we sincerely care!

The disciples also experienced another unexpected change; they faced a time of struggle with their faith. By this I am not implying that they no longer believed that Jesus was the Son of God or that they doubted, for example, what He had accomplished on the cross. However, not having Him physically present with them to answer their questions and calm their fears was not an easy adjustment! They longed for His reassurance—to hear His voice again, telling them all would be well. It is understandable that the faith of these men would be put to the test!

For you and me, when we are confronted by change through the loss of a loved one or some other heartache, our faith may seem weak for a time; we may even wonder if God is really there after all, or if He is, does He truly care about us. Let me assure you, my friend, circumstances in your life may have changed, but God has not changed! God Himself was speaking in the following verse from the Old Testament; He said, "For I am the LORD, I change not" (Malachi 3:6). He is still very near, and He cares for you! Do not allow your heartbreak to distort your view of God or to cause your faith in His love and His ability to meet your needs to waver. Purpose in your heart that the changes you are facing will draw you closer to the Lord Jesus Christ!

A third area of change the disciples encountered was a change in their perspective of life. Up until the time of Christ's arrest in the Garden of Gethsemane, and especially His crucifixion, the disciples' perspective of life reflected a childlike simplicity of heart and an innocence, as they no doubt believed that their time with the Lord would never end—that life would continue exactly as it was, filled with the blessings of being in the presence of Jesus! They would spend the rest of their lives traveling about with Him as He preached the Gospel and performed miracles.

You and I may be journeying through life with that same simplicity of heart; I think especially as young adults we may feel that we are invincible and that we will realize the fulfillment of all our dreams and goals. Unfortunately, sorrow and heartache can strike suddenly from out of nowhere, and we encounter changes that we never believed would happen to us. Instead of fulfilling a dream, our life for a time is more like a nightmare, and that simplicity of heart—that sweet innocence that thinks life will be perfect, is suddenly swept away.

When you and I encounter such a drastic change in our perspective of life, we need to allow God to work in our hearts and use those circumstances, harsh as they may be, to give us wisdom, as well as a greater understanding of ourselves, of life, and especially of God. I have discovered in my own life that in addition to these benefits of encountering heartbreaking changes, I feel that the Lord has used my circumstances to give me more compassion for the needs of others, and also a greater appreciation of my blessings. Once again, we must strive to stay close to the Lord through reading His Word and spending time in prayer; otherwise, the difficult changes that come our way may result in a cynical attitude toward life as well as a critical spirit that will hurt us and others around us.

The disciples also had to deal with change in their daily activities along with the dilemma of something they had taken for granted: the passing of time! When Christ had walked among them, life centered around ministry, and life was busy! There were times when the Lord showed them they needed to rest, but then the excitement and labor of ministering to others with their Lord would resume. It was wonderful! Now suddenly there were no multitudes following them, no lame people being healed, no funeral processions interrupted while Jesus restored a loved one to his family. The disciples' minds and bodies were not active with the excitement of ministry, and there were days that time seemed meaningless as it dragged by. The Lord knew that the disciples had experienced a sudden barrage of changes, and He was patient with them. He knew that they would soon overcome these challenges and would become active in the work of God again, preaching the Gospel and encouraging other believers.

The Lord is patient with His children today as well; He realizes that the changes we experience can affect our desire to engage in our usual activities. Many days we may feel restless; we are missing that sense of purpose—that zest for life— we had before our orderly world was turned into chaos.

My friend, while you are continuing your journey of healing, set some goals and priorities for yourself, so that once they are completed you will have a sense of accomplishment. Some of these should relate to physical activity, such as walking or some other activity you have enjoyed in the past; exercise strengthens our bodies and is an effective way to relieve stress! Other goals should deal with emotions and relationships, and could include not only getting together with friends for an evening of fun, but also talking with that specific friend who has wisdom from God: one who will listen and advise but not publicize! We must not sulk or withdraw from people; instead, it is essential that we become active again!

In regard to time, we gradually need to reclaim it rather than watching the hours slowly pass. Of primary importance (as we have already alluded to earlier) is actually scheduling time with the Lord every day; we need to keep those "appointments" with Him and allow Him to minister to our emotional needs.

My friend, by God's grace and with wisdom and strength from Him, be determined that the changes you encounter will not defeat you! As you spend time with the Lord each day, He will enable you to face each change with faith and perseverance. One day you will be able to help someone else who is struggling with change!

God bless you on your journey!

Hope for Hurting Hearts Journal

Day 20: Encountering Change

Date:_____

Today's Scripture: Psalm 112

"Do not allow your heartbreak to distort your view of God, or to cause your faith in His love and His ability to meet your needs to waver. Purpose in your heart that the changes you are facing will draw you closer to the Lord Jesus Christ!"

*From today's reading I learned:*_____

_____

_____

_____

_____

_____

*On my heart today:*_____

_____

_____

~ Day 21 ~

There Remains More Land to Possess

~ Your Journey Ahead ~

Do you enjoy traveling on a sunny day, just "unwinding" and enjoying God's amazing creation all around you? I have discovered that much of the pleasure of traveling is not just arriving at the final destination, but looking ahead at the beautiful scenery as it unfolds before me. The panorama of mountains, rivers, trees, and flowers does not remain constant throughout the journey, which adds to the enjoyment. Even the canopy of sky overhead varies; at times it resembles an azure sea with islands of fluffy white, then with little notice the azure deepens into indigo, lit up here and there with flashes of lightning. As we travel a few more miles we may be greeted by a rainbow, the colors first vibrant, then fading, then vanishing altogether. If we do not look ahead, there is so much we could miss! I traveled a great deal during the years that I was an evangelist; I enjoyed both the unknown surroundings and the familiar. When I was heading home after a meeting, I knew the way so well that I could predict the next landmark or scenic spot; I could even picture each one in my mind before I saw it coming into view.

My friend, wherever you may be on your journey of healing, or your journey of life, I want to encourage you to look ahead! There are many lovely sights that lie ahead for you, as well as many blessings that the Lord has planned for your future! Yes, you and I need to know where we are right now in our journey as well. We live in the present, and there are people who need us in the present; there are challenges that require our attention and blessings we do not want to miss! However, looking ahead on our journey brings hope and excitement; consequently, we need a balance of both in our lives.

The children of Israel had claimed and settled much of the Promised Land under the leadership of Joshua. However, God spoke these words to him regarding his journey in Joshua 13:1-2:

> 1) *Now Joshua was old and stricken in years; and the LORD said unto him, Thou art old and stricken in years, and there remaineth yet very much land to be possessed.*
> 2) *This is the land that yet remaineth. . . .*

Although Joshua had aged considerably since he was first chosen by God to lead His people, the Lord challenged Him to look ahead, because *"there remaineth yet very much land to be possessed."* Joshua's journey was not over just yet!

Years before this, the Lord had also spoken to the previous leader of the children of Israel, Moses, about certain events that were going to take place—including the fact that Joshua would be the new leader of His people. Let's look at Deuteronomy 31:14-16a, as well as Deuteronomy 32:49, 52.

14) *And the LORD said unto Moses, Behold thy days approach that thou must die: call Joshua, and present yourselves in the tabernacle of the congregation, that I may give him a charge. And Moses and Joshua went, and presented themselves in the tabernacle of the congregation.*
15) *And the LORD appeared in the tabernacle in a pillar of a cloud: and the pillar of the cloud stood over the door of the tabernacle.*
16) *And the LORD said unto Moses, Behold, thou shalt sleep with thy fathers;*
49) *Get thee up into this mountain Abarim, unto mount Nebo, which is in the land of Moab, that is over against Jericho; and behold the land of Canaan, which I give unto the children of Israel for a possession:*
52) *Yet thou shalt see the land before thee; but thou shalt not go thither unto*

the land which I give the children of Israel.

For many years now Moses, Joshua, Caleb, and the remnant of the children of Israel (those who had not doubted God's ability to give them victory over the inhabitants of the land of Canaan) had traveled together through the wilderness; now they stood virtually at the border of the Promised Land. This should have been a time of joyous celebration, but because of Moses' disobedience in smiting the rock to obtain water, instead of speaking to the rock as God had commanded, this day was bittersweet. God informed Joshua and his predecessor that Moses had reached the end of his journey; he would not be accompanying them to the Promised Land. Instead, he would be climbing to the top of Mt. Nebo, where he could see the land promised to the nation of Israel before he died.

This would have been a difficult time for Joshua as well as Moses. They had traveled together for forty years and they had witnessed God do miraculous things. The thought of continuing the journey without Moses no doubt caused Joshua much sadness; the two men had probably grown very close over the years.

Perhaps you have been reading and journaling through this book because you, like Joshua, suddenly found yourself on life's journey without someone you loved dearly—a fellow "traveler" that had been an important part of your journey. If that is the case, you are facing one of the loneliest of all experiences, and my heart goes out to you. I want to do my very best to point you to the Word of God in order to shine the light of hope upon your circumstances, and to help you find the strength that you will need for your journey ahead. I also want to encourage you that, just as it was true of Joshua, so it is for you: *"There remaineth yet very much land to be possessed."*

What I am going to say next may seem harsh, but that is not my intention. My friend, your life is not over! You must continue on your journey! God has left you here for a reason, and He wants you to accomplish something for His glory! Even though you have suffered a great loss and your heart is heavy, God still has a plan for your life. He will give you the wisdom and strength to fulfill that plan, and He will walk with you to the end of your journey.

When God spoke to Joshua, He spoke firmly and with a voice of authority: *"Thou art old and stricken in years, and there remaineth yet very much land to be possessed."* These words could apply to many different circumstances. The word "stricken" implies that Joshua was affected by his age. You, too, have been "stricken" or affected by your circumstances—perhaps by the loss of a loved one, or some other heartbreak. However, you must look at the road ahead. Your own journey has not ended. You have much to conquer, much to accomplish, battles to win, victories to experience, and people to love and lead.

As we read this passage and others in the Word of God, it is important that we pay close attention to what God has said. In this case it is significant to notice what God **did not** say to Joshua. When God met with Moses and Joshua, He did not tell them, "Moses you are going to die on Mount Nebo; consequently, Joshua, you and all the children of Israel will have to return to Egypt." No! On the contrary, God told Joshua, *"Be strong and of a good courage: for thou shalt bring the children of Israel into the land which I sware unto them: and I will be with thee"* (Deuteronomy 31:21).

God did not tell Joshua that he would be on his own in leading the people after Moses' death. No! God told Joshua *"I will be with thee."*

God did not tell Joshua that he had good reason to be afraid, because the journey was going to be difficult without Moses' leadership, and they would never make it. No! God told Joshua, *"Be of a good courage."*

My friend, you can confront your challenges, because you are never alone! God told Joshua *"Thou shalt bring the children of Israel into the land";* you must be strong and of good courage, trusting in the One Who has safely brought you this far in your journey! With the strength and courage the Lord supplies, you can finish the journey well, you can win the battles that lie ahead, and you can be an example for the loved ones in your life today who are probably already looking to you to help them to be strong and courageous. Remember: you are not traveling the journey of life alone. As a believer in Jesus Christ you have a Saviour Who promised, *"I will never leave thee, nor forsake thee"* (Hebrews 13:5b).

It is evidence of God's kindness and grace that even though He did not permit Moses to enter the Promised Land, God did permit Moses to see the land, the place that had been his goal ever since God called him to lead His people out of Egypt. I do not believe that it was merely coincidence that God chose Mount Nebo as the place Moses would end his journey; from the top of that mountain he could see a beautiful panoramic view of the Promised Land! I somehow wonder if the voice of the Lord was a little more tender than it had been earlier as He spoke these words to His servant Moses, a man who had served God faithfully and with humility for so many years: *"Get thee up into this mountain Abarim, unto mount Nebo, which is in the land of Moab, that is over against Jericho; and behold the land of Canaan, which I give unto the children of Israel for a possession"* (Deuteronomy 32:49).

I have loved ones who were walking with me along this journey of life, but they were called away. I had an uncle who died when I was only five years old, a close friend when I was seventeen, my father when I was twenty-three, and my baby grandson in more recent years. Nevertheless, I have come to the realization that *"there remaineth yet very much land to be possessed."* I have continued on my journey without those people I have loved. I have crossed my Jordan Rivers, conquered my Jerichos, taken possession of several mountains, and fought some battles.

Have the loved ones who left my side and entered into their rest on "Mount Nebo" observed my victories? Do they see the road that still lies before me? I believe they can! The Bible speaks of "a great cloud of witnesses" (Hebrews 12:1). I believe that cloud of witnesses includes those who traveled on life's journey with me but for whatever reason God saw fit that they leave my side to be with Him. I believe they have been witnesses of my journey thus far, that they will continue to observe as I travel on, and also that they will greet me on the other side.

Let me encourage you, my dear friend, to continue on your journey, because for you *"there remaineth yet very much land to be possessed."* I challenge you to *"Be strong and of good courage"* because the Saviour travels with you!

God bless you! Keep looking ahead, and travel on!

Hope for Hurting Hearts Journal

Day 21: There Remains More Land to Possess

Date:_____

Today's Scripture: Psalm 30

> "With the strength and courage the Lord supplies, you can finish the journey well, you can win the battles that lie ahead, and you can be an example for the loved ones in your life today who are probably already looking to you to help them to be strong and courageous."

*From today's reading I learned:*_____

_____

_____

_____

_____

*On my heart today:*_____

_____

Hope for Hurting Hearts Journal

Day 22

Date:_____

Today's Scripture: Psalm 103

"The hands of Jesus Christ that blessed
the children when they were brought to
Him and that touched many while He
walked on earth, healing them of their
physical, spiritual and emotional
infirmities, can also bring healing to
your grieving heart."

*On my heart today:*_____

_____

_____

_____

_____

_____

_____

_____

_____

_____

Hope for Hurting Hearts Journal

Day 23

Date:_____

Today's Scripture: Psalm 88

"It is prayer that will keep you close to the Lord, it is prayer that will keep your heart and mind focused on the strength of God, and it is prayer that will help you go farther than you think you can go."

*On my heart today:*_____

_____

_____

_____

_____

_____

_____

_____

_____

_____

Hope for Hurting Hearts Journal

Day 24

Date:_____

Today's Scripture: Psalm 119:33-40

"That I may know him, and the power of
his resurrection, and the fellowship of
his suffering, being made conformable
unto his death." Philippians 3:10

*On my heart today:*_____

_____

_____

_____

_____

_____

_____

_____

_____

_____

_____

Hope for Hurting Hearts Journal

Day 25

Date:_____

Today's Scripture: Psalm 19

"I believe the truest form of worship is to
trust God completely, even in the face of
adversity."

*On my heart today:*_____

_____

_____

_____

_____

_____

_____

_____

_____

_____

_____

Hope for Hurting Hearts Journal

Day 26

*Date:*_____

Today's Scripture: Psalm 31

"God cares for you and is able to see you through the most difficult storms, and He will give you strength for the bitter cups of life."

*On my heart today:*_____

_____

_____

_____

_____

_____

_____

_____

_____

_____

_____

Hope for Hurting Hearts Journal

Day 27

Date:_____

Today's Scripture: Psalm 119:1-8

"We will never know this side of Heaven what strength and courage we may give someone else who watched from a distance as we drank from our bitter cup."

*On my heart today:*_____

_____

_____

_____

_____

_____

_____

_____

_____

_____

_____

Hope for Hurting Hearts Journal

Day 28

*Date:*_____

Today's Scripture: Psalm 119:161-168

"Remember that when the Saviour was
betrayed by Judas, He did not retaliate
or attack, but He called the one that
betrayed him 'friend.'"

*On my heart today:*_____

_____

_____

_____

_____

_____

_____

_____

_____

_____

_____

Hope for Hurting Hearts Journal

Day 29

Date:_____

Today's Scripture: Psalm 23

"For a shadow to exist in the valley of the shadow of death there must be a light somewhere."

*On my heart today:*_____

_____

_____

_____

_____

_____

_____

_____

_____

_____

_____

_____

Hope for Hurting Hearts Journal

Day 30

Date:_____

Today's Scripture: Psalm 91

"We can choose to follow our fears and be overcome by them, we can choose defeat and discouragement, or we can choose to commend our spirit to God the Father, and we can choose to trust God."

*On my heart today:*_____

_____

_____

_____

_____

_____

_____

_____

_____

_____

_____

Hope for Hurting Hearts Journal

Day 31

*Date:*_____

Today's Scripture: Psalm 119:57-64

"Your pain will become someone else's
strength. Your surrender to the will of
God will become someone else's
confidence. Your brokenness will
become someone else's healing."

*On my heart today*_____

_____

_____

_____

_____

_____

_____

_____

_____

_____

_____

Day 32

*Date:*_____

Today's Scripture: Psalm 75

"To everything there is a season, and a
time to every purpose under heaven: A
time to be born, and a time to die; A
time to plant, and a time to pluck up
that which is planted; A time to kill, and
a time to heal; A time to break down,
and a time to build up; A time to weep,
and a time to laugh; A time to mourn,
and a time to dance" Ecclesiastes 3:1-4

*On my heart today:*_____

_____

_____

_____

_____

_____

_____

_____

Hope for Hurting Hearts Journal

Day 33

Date:_____

Today's Scripture: Psalm 34

"We must come to a point that we make
a conscious decision to enter into the
season of healing, building up,
laughing, dancing, embracing and
rejoicing."

*On my heart today:*_____

_____

_____

_____

_____

_____

_____

_____

_____

_____

_____

Hope for Hurting Hearts Journal

Day 34

Date:_____

Today's Scripture: Psalm 40

"There is a season to live! The very
action of choosing to laugh, the action of
choosing to be a blessing to others, the
action of finding something to rejoice in
and then rejoicing in that thing, will
help you in your healing journey."

*On my heart today:*_____

_____

_____

_____

_____

_____

_____

_____

_____

_____

Hope for Hurting Hearts Journal

Day 35

*Date:*_____

Today's Scripture: Psalm 41

> Through many dangers, toils and snares
> I have already come;
> 'Tis grace has brought me safe thus far
> And grace will lead me home.
>
> ---John Newton ("Amazing Grace")

*On my heart today:*_____

_____

_____

_____

_____

_____

_____

_____

_____

_____

Hope for Hurting Hearts Journal

Day 36

Date:_____

Today's Scripture: Psalm 126

"The gracious God of Heaven will
someday take you into His arms and
will wipe all tears from your eyes."

*On my heart today:*_____

_____

_____

_____

_____

_____

_____

_____

_____

_____

_____

_____

_____

Hope for Hurting Hearts Journal

Day 37

Date:_____

Today's Scripture: Psalm 77

"Sometimes when we are dealing with a
grieving heart we must be reliant on the
assistance of others."

*On my heart today:*_____

_____

_____

_____

_____

_____

_____

_____

_____

_____

_____

_____

Hope for Hurting Hearts Journal

Day 38

Date:_____

Today's Scripture: Psalm 84

". . . My grace is sufficient for thee: for
my strength is made perfect in
weakness, Most gladly therefore will I
rather glory in my infirmities, that the
power of Christ may rest upon me."
II Corinthians 12:9

*On my heart today:*_____

_____

_____

_____

_____

_____

_____

_____

_____

_____

Hope for Hurting Hearts Journal

Day 39

*Date:*_____

Today's Scripture: Psalm 108

"No journey is complete that does not lead through some dark valleys. We can properly comfort others only wherewith we ourselves have been comforted of God." Vance Havner

*On my heart today:*_____

_____

_____

_____

_____

_____

_____

_____

_____

_____

_____

Hope for Hurting Hearts Journal

Day 40

Date:_____

Today's Scripture: Psalm 106

"Let me encourage you, my dear friend, to continue on your journey, because for you *'there remaineth yet very much land to be possessed.'* I challenge you to *'Be strong and of good courage'* because the Saviour travels with you!"

*On my heart today:*_____

_____

_____

_____

_____

_____

_____

_____

_____

~HEAVEN~

Dear Reader:

This book will be of little help to you if you do not have a personal relationship with Jesus Christ. Receiving His free gift of eternal life is the first step to victory in this life, and it is the only way to have eternal life in Heaven.

The Bible says,

"For all have sinned and come short of the glory of God." - Romans 3:23

You and I were born sinners; we have a sin nature, and we have sinned against God in our deeds and thoughts.

"But God commendeth his love toward us, in that while we were yet sinners, Christ died for us." - Romans 5:8

Although we are sinners God loves us, and He gave His only begotten Son, Jesus Christ, to die for our sins in our place. He took our punishment for the sins we have committed.

"For the wages of sin is death; but the gift of God is eternal life through Jesus Christ our Lord." - Romans 6:23

Because we are sinners, we will die; death is the penalty of sin. Death is also separation; if we die without Jesus Christ as our Saviour, we will be separated from God and in Hell for eternity, where we will be punished for our sin. But God's gift to us is eternal life in Heaven with Him forever. In order to have this free gift of eternal life, we must receive it by faith.

"That if thou shalt confess with thy mouth the Lord Jesus, and shalt believe in thine heart that God hath raised Him from the dead, thou shalt be saved. For with the heart man believeth unto righteousness; and with the mouth confession is made unto salvation." -Romans 10:9-10

To confess means to be in agreement. If you agree with the Word of God that you have sinned, and if you believe in your heart that Jesus Christ is the Son of God, that He died for your sins, and that God raised Him from the dead, then you may receive God's free gift of eternal life.

"For whosoever shall call upon the name of the Lord shall be saved." -Romans 10:13

If you have never received God's free gift of eternal life and would like to do so now, turn from your sin and turn to Jesus Christ. Pray sincerely from your heart a prayer similar to this:

Dear God, I confess that I am a sinner; I believe that Jesus Christ died for my sin on the cross. By faith I repent and turn from my sin to Christ. By faith I receive Jesus Christ as my Saviour that I may have eternal life. Lord, help me to live for you. Thank you for saving me and for giving me eternal life. Amen.

If we can be of help to you, please feel free to contact us.

Dr. Don Woodard
Hope for Hurting Hearts
PO Box 490
Troutville, VA 24175
csm2va@netzero.net ~ 540-354-8573

Visit us at

yourhopejourney.org

ALSO AVAILABLE:

When The Will of God is a Bitter Cup . . . $9.00

Marrying the Right One $7.95

Blessings From Parenthood $5.00

Teenager, You Can Make it. $5.00

Reaching Teenagers* $14.00

*(Practical Bible Methods for the Local Church Youth Ministry)

LightKeeper Publications
PO Box 490
Troutville, VA 24175
540-354-8573

~ABOUT THE AUTHOR~

Don Woodard (D.D.) and his wife Debbie, live in Southwest Virginia near Roanoke, have been blessed with five children and six grandchildren. The Woodards have been actively involved in the work of the Lord since 1985; for fifteen years Dr. Woodard traveled as an evangelist and conference speaker. Today he serves as pastor of the Beacon Baptist Church in Salem, Virginia.

Dr. Woodard knows from personal experience the sorrow that accompanies grief and a broken heart. In his book, *Hope for Hurting Hearts*, he guides the reader along a spiritual journey of hope and healing.